EPIC
FAIL

THE ULTIMATE
BOOK OF BLUNDERS

MARK LEIGH

4 6 8 10 9 7 5

First published in the UK in 2013 by Virgin Books,
an imprint of Ebury Publishing

A Random House Group Company

Copyright © Virgin Books 2013

Illustrations by Andrew Pinder

www.randomhouse.co.uk

Addresses for companies within The Random House Group Limited
can be found at www.randomhouse.co.uk/offices.htm

The Random House Group Limited Reg. No. 954009

A CIP catalogue record for this book is available from the British Library.

www.randomhouse.co.uk/environment

Designed and typeset by K.DESIGN, Winscombe, Somerset

ISBN: 9780753541265

To buy books by your favourite authors and register for offers,
visit www.randomhouse.co.uk

The Random House Group Limited supports The Forest Stewardship
Council® (FSC®), the leading international forest-certification organisation.
Our books carrying the FSC label are printed on FSC®-certified paper.
FSC is the only forest-certification scheme supported by the leading
environmental organisations, including Greenpeace. Our
paper procurement policy can be found at
www.randomhouse.co.uk/environment

Printed and bound in Great Britain by Clays Ltd, St Ives plc

*'Sometimes failure isn't an opportunity
in disguise, it's just you.'*

DOUG COUPLAND

ABOUT THE AUTHOR

Mark Leigh is superbly qualified to write this book, having failed miserably in his quest to marry a lingerie model, invent a machine that turns earwax into gold or discover a cure for male pattern baldness. His accomplishments however include writing or co-writing forty-five humour titles on subjects as diverse as celebrities, extra-terrestrials, swearing pets and toilets, as well as a comedy novel *Dick Longg: Sexual Saviour of the Universe!* (available on Kindle). Mark lives in Surrey with his family and when he's not writing or failing, works in marketing and plays bass in his death metal group Blunt Force Trauma.

For more details visit **www.mark-leigh.com**

CONTENTS

INTRODUCTION

> *'If at first you don't succeed, failure might be your style.'*
>
> QUENTIN CRISP

There's nothing that quite tickles the funny bone like the proverbial banana slip. Seeing people fall on their arse carries the sort of guilty amusement that sees us both sniggering and secretly thinking 'thank God it wasn't me'.

Some might try to dignify these epic fails by claiming they're the path to glory or that there's a sense of nobility about them. Bullshit! There's nothing heroic or glorious about failing – just ask the guy who attempted to recreate *that* scene from *American Pie* and landed himself in a burns unit... From the hundreds of examples in this book, it's clear that failure isn't a speed bump on the road to success; it's embarrassing, humiliating and nearly always results in abject shame or serious bodily harm.

Whether it's life's way of telling you you're in the shallow end of the gene pool or it's just plain bad luck, failure in ourselves is depressing, but in others it never fails to amuse.

So sit back, kick off your shoes and enjoy this compilation of epic fails, including the courthouse that used a Danielle

Steele romance instead of the Bible to swear oaths, and the terrorist who failed to put enough postage on his letter bomb, thus ensuring it came back to him marked 'Return to sender'...

Mistakes, mishaps and the world's biggest balls-ups... You'll find them all here in *Epic Fail*.

Mark Leigh, 2013

HISTORIC EPIC FAILS

> *'Never interrupt your enemy when he is making a mistake.'*
> NAPOLEON BONAPARTE

Ever since Eve thought listening to a talking snake was a good idea, humans have suffered epic lapses of judgement. History may be written by the victors, but luckily for us, the victors take great satisfaction in writing about the losers...

King Gustavus Adolphus of Sweden wanted his navy to have the world's largest warship, and so in 1626 construction began on the *Vasa*. Two years later the 226-foot-long vessel set sail on its maiden voyage from Stockholm carrying 145 sailors, 300 soldiers and 64 guns. Within ten minutes it had keeled over, filled with water and sank.

The death of Franz Ferdinand, Archduke of Austria, the event that precipitated the First World War, can be put down to his vanity. Rather than allow any wrinkles to be visible in his uniform, he was sewn into his military tunic. After he was shot alongside his wife in Sarajevo in June 1914, those coming to his rescue were unable to reach his wounds, as they couldn't locate any buttons on his uniform. By the time they managed to cut him out of his clothes he was dead.

Adolf Hitler took sleeping pills on the night of 5 June 1944 and gave instructions that he was not to be woken under any circumstances. At dawn the next day Allied forces landed on the Normandy coast and the D-Day invasion began. Field Marshal von Rundstedt ordered two Panzer divisions to head to the region but was told to stand down by the German command in Berlin until he received direct orders from the Führer himself. Hitler didn't wake up until midday – by which time the Allies had established their positions and were beginning to advance.

In 1915 the Mexican revolutionary lieutenant Rodolfo Fierro was marching with Pancho Villa's troops towards the town of Sonora when he decided to take a shortcut. His horse was spooked en route and threw Fierro from its saddle into quicksand. Weighed down by the sizeable amount of looted gold coins he was carrying, Fierro slowly sank to his death.

Marie Antoinette and her husband, King Louis XVI, were captured trying to leave Paris during the French Revolution as they changed horses at the town of Varennes in 1791. Although dressed as commoners, Mme Antoinette had forgotten one part of her disguise: she was still wearing her pungent Houbigant perfume – a smell far too rich for any of the lower classes to be wearing. Captured, they were forced to remain in the city until their eventual executions in 1793.

FAIL

The composer Irving Berlin had a huge hit with 'White Christmas', written in 1940. It became something of a morale-boosting song for Allied troops, and eventually led him to visit Great Britain. One of Winston Churchill's aides mentioned that Mr Berlin was in the country and the prime minister immediately asked him to set up a special reception for the great man.

Irving Berlin was honoured and amazed when he found himself actually sitting next to Churchill at the lunch. Throughout the meal Churchill kept probing him about the war and what he would do if he were in the PM's shoes.

Berlin felt out of his depth – he was a composer, not a politician or a military strategist, and all he could offer were short, glib, noncommittal answers. After the lunch and the goodbyes Churchill turned to his wife and commented on how thoughtful his special guest was, so unassuming and lacking in pomposity, considering he was one of the world's leading thinkers... Churchill thought he'd invited *Isaiah* Berlin, the great philosopher.

In 1521 the explorer Ferdinand Magellan crossed the Pacific Ocean without encountering any bad weather and named it *Mar Pacifico*, meaning 'peaceful sea' in Portuguese. Nothing could be further from the truth; the Pacific Ocean is home to some of the most devastating typhoons, tidal waves and storms on the planet.

Cesare Borgia's wedding night was an epic fail. When he married the French Princess Charlotte d'Albret in 1499, his so-called friends jokingly swapped his aphrodisiacs for powerful laxatives. Court gossip at the time said any amorous intentions he might have had were wrecked by eight trips to the palace privy.

Jean-Pierre Blanchard was a pioneering French aeronaut, crossing the English Channel in a hot-air balloon in 1785 and giving the first demonstration of a parachute in the same year. His wife, Sophie, however, goes down in history as someone not quite as heroic... or, in fact, bright. After a successful balloon ascent over Paris on her own in July 1819, she decided to celebrate by letting off some fireworks she had brought with her. Needless to say, one of them set fire to the balloon, causing it and Madame Blanchard to plummet fatally to the ground from a great height.

Francis Bacon, the sixteenth-century author, philosopher, statesman and scientist, had a restlessly inquisitive mind. In 1626, he decided to investigate ways of preserving food by freezing it. One of his experiments involved stuffing a dead goose (some accounts say it was a hen) full of snow, leaving it for a while and then eating it. The result – the conclusion that this was not a good method of preserving meat – came at a high personal cost... he caught typhoid and pneumonia and died.

Italian astrologer Gerolamo Cardano studied the movement of the planets and predicted the exact date of his own death: 21 September 1576. When the day came Cardano found himself in the best of health and the fact he was still alive meant his reputation as an accurate predictor of the future was now in doubt. He was so distressed by this thought that he killed himself.

[FAIL]

The Lord Mayor of London did not take kindly to being roused from his bed in the early hours of 2 September 1666 and taken to see a small fire that had broken out at a bakery in Pudding Lane. After complaining about his ruined sleep, he returned home, stating, 'Pish! A woman might piss it out.' The ensuing Great Fire of London destroyed 87 churches and over 13,000 houses.

In 1519 the Aztec ruler Montezuma II welcomed Hernando Cortés to Mexico, convinced he was the exiled wind god Quetzalcoatl. He welcomed the Spanish conquistador with lavish gifts of gold and silver. In return Cortes introduced smallpox, which devastated the Aztec empire.

In 1880, hearing about the latest method of executing criminals, Emperor Menelik II of Ethiopia ordered three electric chairs to be shipped from New York. What he failed to realize, however, was that the electric chairs required electricity to work (he missed the clue in the name) and Ethiopia did not have electrical power at the time. The emperor ended up using one of the chairs as his throne.

John Warburton (1682–1759) devoted much of his life – and a good part of his fortune – to collecting rare and antiquarian books. The pride of his collection was 58 first-edition plays, including many of Shakespeare's original works. He came home one day to find that his cook, Betsy Baker, had mistaken them for waste paper and had either used them to light fires or line pie pans. Only three survived.

King Charles II of France died as an indirect result of a cure for leprosy. After he had contracted the disease the royal doctors recommended that he be wrapped in cloth that had been soaked in a mixture of sulphur and alcohol. This was thought to cure his skin condition – and might well have if a clumsy page hadn't accidentally set fire to the bandages, burning the king alive.

FAIL

The famed Danish astronomer Tycho Brahe (1546–1601) quite literally had his head in the stars just before an important state banquet. He forgot to go to the lavatory, an act that would have disastrous consequences. At the time it was considered impolite and insulting to the host if you left the table before the meal was over. Brahe desperately wanted to go but had to suffer in silence. The result of his good manners was a burst bladder, followed by his painful death 11 days later.

[FAIL]

No matter how grand it is or how much money you spend on it, even the best-laid weddings sometimes don't go according to plan. In 1867 Princess Maria dal Pozzo della Cisterna married Amadeo, the Duke of D'Aosta and heir to the Italian throne. On the wedding day her wardrobe mistress hanged herself, the palace gatekeeper cut his throat, the station-master was crushed under the wheels of the honeymoon train and the king's aide died falling from his horse. Oh yes – and the best man shot himself.

King Philip III of Spain met a rather inglorious end as the direct result of overzealous palace officials adhering too closely to royal etiquette.

During a meeting with his ministers it was evident that the king was having breathing difficulties caused by fumes from a charcoal heater in the room.

It soon became obvious that the king was having real trouble breathing – but no one would take responsibility for removing the brazier. Unfortunately the official whose job it was to look after the heater was not present, and everyone else felt it would not be protocol if they did his job.

While they agonized, King Philip died of asphyxiation.

PLAIN BAD LUCK

It's said that bad luck makes for great stories. Based on the evidence of these spectacular fails, it's hard to disagree...

The Reverend Roy Briggs was a great fan of poet Rupert Brooke and especially his poem, 'The Old Vicarage, Grantchester'. Although living in Johannesburg, in April 1993 he decided to make an expensive pilgrimage to the village in Cambridgeshire – nearly 9,000 miles away – to photograph the famous clock described in the poem:

'Stands the church clock at ten to three?
And is there honey still for tea?'

He arrived in the village, excitedly found the vicarage as described and was about to take the photo when he noticed the clock had stopped at five past one.

FAIL

Paperwork delayed an Arizona couple's divorce by 11 days. In that time, the husband won $2.2 million (£1.4 million) on the state lottery. Because they were still legally married at that time, the judge ruled the wife was entitled to 25 per cent of his winnings.

[FAIL]

In 1994 Conrado Bacani won a second-hand car in a raffle in his native Philippines, but when he tried to register it, he was arrested for being in possession of a stolen car. It turned out that the car was previously reported stolen and had never been recovered.

Sal Aspione from Sassari in Italy wanted to make his proposal to his girlfriend, Sara Rizzi, memorable, so over an expensive dinner in 1992 he slipped an engagement ring into her glass of Champagne. Unfortunately she failed to see the ring and choked to death on it. Aspione later commented, 'I wanted to do something special for the woman I loved.'

17

In 1994 Dale Miller of Florida bought a winning lottery ticket worth $6.6 million. Before he collected his jackpot he celebrated this life-changing win by getting drunk and then ending up in a huge argument with his wife. He stormed out but returned home the next day only to find that his wife, feeling guilty about the row, had tidied their house from top to bottom, accidentally throwing out the winning ticket in the process. Miller spent two weeks searching the local garbage tip for the ticket – without success. In the process he was asked what he'd spend his winnings on, should he ever find the ticket. He replied, 'Clean clothes and a divorce.'

Two Polish 17-year-olds, Beata and Kamil, were forbidden by their parents from marrying, so, inspired by Romeo and Juliet, decided it would be better to live together for eternity in death rather than be separated in life. They went to a chemist to buy a strong poison but the pharmacist became suspicious and instead sold them a bottle of the strongest laxative.

The couple booked into an economy room in a local hotel – a room without a toilet and bathroom, and shared the 'poison' before laying on the bed in each other's arms. It wasn't long before the laxative started to work. Having no toilet was one thing but the couple had no means to find another bathroom – as part of their plan they had locked their room and thrown the key out of the window.

All they could do was scream for help – help that arrived too late.

The hotel manager had to fumigate the room afterwards and commented that the couple had found each other so disgusting that they called off their engagement.

Scott Wenner of Texas won $10 million on the state lottery – and then was told that his winning ticket was forfeit because the shop he'd bought it from was unlicensed.

[FAIL]

Susan Evans sent her boyfriend out to get her UK National Lottery ticket. Unfortunately, he got stuck in a queue and the lottery closed just as the ticket was being processed, rendering it invalid. That night, all her numbers came up. A few seconds earlier, and Sue would have won an £8.5 million jackpot.

In 1975 Gustavo Amador, a Honduran peasant, was charged with stealing pencils from a local market but was acquitted the following year. Unfortunately the written release order did not reach the jail in which Gustavo was being held until 19 years later. He was released in 1994.

[FAIL]

In 1992 Salvatore Chirilino reached for a lucky four-leaf clover on a clifftop in Vibo Marina, Italy, when he slipped on the wet grass and fell 150 feet to his death. A police spokesman was quoted as saying (predictably), 'It's just not lucky for everyone.'

Brighton resident Martin Reeves travelled 8,000 miles to India to buy parts for his prized 1957 Morris Cowley (the car was the basis of the locally produced Hindustan Ambassador). His mission was a success, but when he returned home he discovered his car had been stolen.

In Zimbabwe in 1994 a woman arrested by police for shoplifting protested her innocence and stripped to her underwear in order to prove she hadn't stolen any clothes. She hadn't, but was then arrested for indecent exposure.

French gambler Michel LaTruille always blew on dice for luck just before he threw them. Unfortunately, one day at a Paris casino in 1993, he accidentally sucked instead, swallowing the dice and choking to death.

In 1991 65-year-old Chan Wai Fong was standing outside her son's apartment block in Hong Kong thanking the gods for her daughter-in-law's lucky escape from a road accident when she was hit and killed by a bag of cement, dropped by builders working above.

In 1983 a motorist who crashed his car into an electricity pylon in Elm, Cambridge, escaped unharmed. After calling the emergency services he brushed against a live cable that was dangling from the bent pylon and was instantly electrocuted.

A similar fate befell Italian Vittoria Luise, who was out driving during a fierce storm in Naples. A huge gust of wind blew his car into the River Sele, but as the car began to sink the calm motorist managed to break a window and swim to safety. He dragged himself on to the riverbank and it was here that he was hit by a falling tree and killed.

A professional French pickpocket chose the wrong victim when he dipped into a bag next to a group of young men waiting at Seville Airport in August 1999. It belonged to Larry Wade, the US champion 110-metres hurdler. He was also spotted by his colleague, Maurice Greene, then the fastest sprinter in the world, with a time of 9.79 seconds for the 100 metres. They didn't take long to apprehend the French thief.

A Torquay bowling club called in exterminators to get rid of wild rabbits that were severely damaging its greens. At the end of the process the exterminators had only managed to trap and kill one rabbit: the club's mascot, Lucky. Players at the club had adopted the animal when they were on a losing streak and it was credited with turning their fortunes around. After Lucky's death the bad results returned.

FAIL

In 1980 Mrs Maureen Wilcox of Massachusetts thought she'd double her chances of winning a fortune by entering both the Massachusetts and Rhode Island state lotteries, with a different set of numbers for each. Defying the odds, in the same week both her numbers came up in both lotteries. She would have won two jackpots – except for the fact that her Massachusetts numbers came up on the Rhode Island lottery and her Rhode Island numbers were the winning combination on the Massachusetts lottery.

An 82-year-old New Zealander named Richard Morsted suffered from severe facial spasms. While out one night in Auckland he was arrested for trying to pick up a prostitute. His constant winking and nodding was interpreted by police as an attempt to attract the attention of the local ladies of the night.

Frank Perkins of Los Angeles attempted to break the world record for flagpole sitting in 1992, but after returning to the ground after 400 days he realized he was actually eight days short of the record. In addition, his sponsor had gone bust, his electricity had been cut off – and his girlfriend had left him.

[FAIL]

In a mammoth piece of detective work, 43-year-old Ian Lewis of Standish, Lancashire, spent 30 years methodically tracing his family tree back to the seventeenth century. In the course of his research he travelled all over the UK talking to over 1,000 distant relatives and planned to write a book about how his great-grandfather had left England to seek his fortune in Russia and how his grandfather was expelled after the Revolution. Then he discovered it had all been in vain; he had been adopted when he was just a month old and his birth name was actually David Thornton.

In February 1996, a 20-year-old drug dealer in Omaha, Nebraska, paged a customer but misdialled and, by chance, reached undercover narcotics officer Sergeant Mark Langan. Langan realized from the terminology being used that he was in touch with a dealer, set up a meeting to buy some crack cocaine – and promptly made his arrest.

ACCIDENTS WILL HAPPEN

> *'Failure is simply the opportunity to begin again, this time more intelligently.'*
>
> HENRY FORD

When it comes to accidents some blame karma, fate or divine intervention. That's fine, but don't underestimate the fact that some people do very stupid things...

The Mayor of Candaba in the northern Philippines used to show off by swaggering around with a loaded pistol in his belt. One day in 1985 he'd just got into his official car when the gun accidentally discharged as he sat down. His driver rushed him to the hospital but ran out of petrol en route and the mayor bled to death..

FAIL

In April 1994 Tamara Klemkowsky, 32, of Waldorf, Maryland, was hospitalized with broken bones after falling from a chartered bus returning from a bachelorette party. Deciding to add some more fun to the festivities she'd dropped her trousers and mooned a passing car. In the process her bottom had pushed against an emergency window that gave way, sending Tamara sprawling on to the highway from the speeding bus.

⟨FAIL⟩

In September 1987 the operators of High Marnham power station on the River Trent in Nottinghamshire decided to celebrate their record of 100 accident-free days by flying a special commemorative flag. As this was proudly being hoisted the pulley wheel fell off, striking a security guard on the head.

Bobby Leach from Cornwall had a reputation as a daredevil. In July 1911 he became the first man and the second person to go over the Niagara Falls in a barrel (he spent six months recovering from his injuries). Ironically his death came not from attempting any more stunts, but after slipping on an orange peel on a publicity tour in New Zealand.

⟨FAIL⟩

To make sure his mother-in-law's house was ready for the festivities, Richard Gardner decided to carry out some DIY at her home in Lancaster, South Carolina, on Christmas Eve 1995. Not having a hammer to hand he decided to use the next best thing: the handle of his empty pistol. It turned out the pistol wasn't empty after all, and as he hit the first nail, Gardner shot himself in the hand and his wife in the stomach.

Marion Fergusson, 42, was walking past the offices of Swinton Insurance in Ormskirk when she was hit by a heavy sign that had worked loose of its hinges. As a result of the accident Marion had to spend three weeks in hospital recovering from four broken ribs and a bad cut to her head. The sign that hit her was advertising accident insurance.

Until July 1994, it was the custom at the Adria textile factory in Strabane, Northern Ireland, for grooms-to-be to be tied to a gate, stripped to their underpants and doused with a bucket of soap slops. When employee David Friel screamed more than the average victim, it was obvious that something was seriously wrong. It was soon discovered that the bucket had mistakenly been filled with industrial caustic soda. Mr Friel suffered 70 per cent burns and missed his own wedding.

FAIL

It's never good when pilots fight, especially when they're in the process of landing an airliner containing 152 passengers. That's what happened, though, in 1994 when Korean Air pilot Barry Edward Woods and co-pilot Chung Chan-kyu started arguing about whether the runway in the southern resort of Cheju was long enough.

The pair fought each other for control of the aircraft, causing it to skid off the runway and into a safety barrier. All the passengers and crew escaped down emergency chutes moments before the Airbus A300 was rocked by multiple explosions and burst into flames.

Grigory Romanov was one of the wealthiest and most influential Russians under the old Soviet regime. As a senior member of the Politburo and Mayor of Moscow, he was able to use his influence to get hold of virtually anything. When his daughter got married In June 1980 he was able to call up the director of Moscow's Hermitage Museum and ask to borrow Catherine the Great's priceless and exquisite china dinner service for use at the wedding. Naturally, he got his way and the dinner service was delivered to the wedding reception.

Later in the evening a guest accidentally dropped one of the delicate teacups. Consequently, the entire reception assumed that they were being asked to make a traditional Russian toast and hurled the crockery into the fireplace.

In December 2009 Vladimir Likhonos, a 25-year-old Ukrainian chemistry student, accidentally dipped his chewing gum in a mixture of explosives he was using in his studies rather than the citric acid that he used to enhance the gum's sour taste. Chewing on the gum caused an explosion that blew off his jaw and most of his lower face. A police spokesperson said, 'Anybody could have mixed them up.'

In 1988 two New York lawyers were arguing over the time for the Olympic 100-metre record when they decided to time themselves running down one of the longest corridors in their office. One of the lawyers wasn't wearing his contact lenses at the time and continued after the 100-metre mark had been passed – flying out of a 39th-floor window to his death.

[FAIL]

A dinner for some of New York's most devoted wine-buffs that took place in April 1989 at Manhattan's Four Seasons restaurant was the perfect opportunity for wine merchant William Sokolin to show off his prized possession: a bottle of 1787 Château Margaux that once belonged to President Thomas Jefferson and which was valued at $519,000 (£324,000). Mr Sokolin was carrying the bottle when he walked into a table, smashing it. He was forced to watch helplessly as the wine gushed out, soaking the rug.

In 1991 18-year-old Roberto Lorenzato was visiting the castle of San Giovanni in the province of Piacenza, Italy, when he asked his fiancée, Stefani Ferrazza, to step back so he could fit her in the frame as he took her photograph. She did so and tumbled 50 feet to her death off the battlement wall.

In 1976 the British Aircraft Corporation produced a safety film for employees at their Preston factory to stress the importance of wearing protective goggles at all times – and the consequences if you didn't. The film was so shocking and graphic that during the first screenings 13 members of staff had to leave the room. A welder fell off his chair and needed seven stitches while a group of machinists, considered the most macho of all the trades, became so nauseous they, too, had to be led out. The film was later withdrawn for 'safety reasons'.

In 1995, Danny Wyman was out on Fox Lake, Illinois, with a fishing buddy, confident of his success. Rather than rely on traditional rods and lines, the pair had taken with them a high-powered firework known as an M-250, infamous for delivering the same explosive power as a quarter of a stick of dynamite. They lit the M-250 and threw it in the lake, waiting for the blast to stun or kill a whole boatload of fish. Unfortunately a gust of wind blew their aluminium rowing boat directly over the firework when it exploded.

Danny's friend managed to scrabble to shore but Danny couldn't swim – and since the pair hadn't taken any life vests with them, he went down with the boat.

In March 2001 the UK's Public Health Laboratory Service held an important conference on food poisoning and water-borne infection in Colindale, north London.

Thirty of the 78 attendees went down with food poisoning. To add insult to injury a spokesman commented, 'It might have been a water-borne infection.'

[FAIL]

Idiots and guns are a lethal combination. . .

Herbert Kershaw, a 59-year-old minister from Enfield, New Hampshire, had just attended a firearms course and was pointing out the safety features of his new .45-calibre pistol not realizing the gun was loaded, when it went off, killing him.

Gaston Lyle Senac, 20, of Tracy, California, was showing friends how rock star Kurt Cobain had killed himself by propping a shotgun on the floor and putting his mouth over the barrel. According to police he said, 'Look, I'm just like Kurt Cobain' – then the gun accidentally went off.

At a stag party in Cosenza, Italy, in August 1997, guests were curious and somewhat annoyed when a stripper they'd hired to leap out of a giant cake failed to make her appearance. Assuming she was no longer in there, they received a nasty shock when they found her dead inside it. Gina Lalapola, 23, had suffocated after waiting for an hour inside the sealed cake.

[FAIL]

David Vasquez of Sacramento, California, decided to have some fun with an illegal firework renowned for its immense explosive power. Driving in his car one day in 1993 he lit it and threw it out of the open window. Unfortunately for him the firework hit the wlndow frame and bounced back in the footwell, between his legs. Seconds later it exploded, severely damaging his testicles.

While recovering in the UC Davis Medical Center, Vasquez commented, 'It messed me up pretty bad.'

JUST PLAIN DUMB

> *'Behind every failure there is an opportunity somebody wishes they had missed.'*
>
> LILY TOMLIN

Albert Einstein said, 'Two things are infinite: the universe and human stupidity; and I'm not sure about the universe.' He called that right...

When his car's fuel line froze, 23-year-old George Gibbs of Columbus, Ohio, decided there was only one thing to do: heat up a two-gallon container of petrol on his stove and use the warm fuel to free the blockage.

The outcome was somewhat predictable, involving an inevitable visit from local firefighters who attempted to save his house.

Guitarist Terry Kath, a founding member of the band Chicago, died during a game of Russian roulette at a party at his roadie's house in 1978. His last words as he held the 9mm semi-automatic pistol to his head were, 'Don't worry. It's not loaded.'

A 25-year-old poacher in the Russian town of Tula wasn't the brightest spark when he had the idea of putting a live electrical cable into a pond to kill fish. It worked, but the authorities who later found his electrocuted body think he forgot to disconnect the current before wading into the water to collect his catch.

[FAIL]

Atlanta Braves pitcher John Smoltz was treated for five-inch-long welts after he tried to iron his shorts while wearing them. He commented, 'I've ironed that way five or six times and never had it happen before.'

While trying to recreate *that* scene from *American Pie* in March 2000, 17-year-old Dwight Emberger got more than a little hot under the collar. Failing to let the pie cool down enough Dwight was rushed to hospital suffering serious burns to his penis.

[FAIL]

Iraqi terrorist Khay Rahnajet failed to put enough postage on the letter bomb he dispatched. It came back marked 'Return to sender' and Rahnajet, forgetting that he'd sent it, opened it. The bomb worked as planned.

In 1978, 55-year-old American crime/mystery writer Jack Drummond was working on a new book titled *Bank Robber*. He decided there only one way to ensure maximum authenticity for the story: he would experience first-hand what it would actually be like to rob a bank.

Drummond sent a copy of his notes to his daughter, warning her that he might soon be in a lot of trouble in the name of research. He was right. Drummond entered a bank in Columbus, Ohio, and had just had time to make his demands and draw a pistol when he was shot dead by a security guard.

Vicki Childress, 38, of Key West, Florida, slept with both a handgun and her asthma inhaler under her pillow. One night in 1991 she suffered an asthma attack and in the dark reached for the wrong item, firing a bullet into her jaw.

A farmer in São Paulo, Brazil, needed to remove a beehive from an orange tree in 2002 and had an ingenious way to avoid being stung in the process. Not having proper beekeeping protective clothing he covered up all his exposed skin, and to protect his face from stings he wore a clear plastic bag over his head, sealing it tightly with tape at his neck. After he failed to return from his mission his wife found him dead at the hive. He'd forgotten to put any air holes in the bag.

In 1976 a Mr D. Beenan of New Zealand decided to protest against hanging, which was still in force in his country at that time. His protest consisted of him putting a noose around his neck and acting out a hanging in order to demonstrate just how barbaric it was. Tragically, in the process he managed to hang himself.

[FAIL]

Even though his friends had attached a heavy ball and chain to the leg of 22-year-old David Godin on his stag night, he decided to drive back to his home in Nova Scotia with it still attached. He would have made it back safely had his car not plunged into a lake, and the weight of the ball not prevented him from swimming to the surface.

Tony Roberts was so keen on joining the Mountain Men Anonymous rafting club in Grant's Pass, Oregon, that he happily agreed to the initiation rite of having an apple shot off his head, William Tell-style. The problem was that the shooter was drunk at the time and aimed a little too low. The arrow pierced Tony's right eye, penetrated his brain and exited though the back of his skull. Although he lost his eye the arrow was successfully removed from his brain with no apparent ill effects. Roberts later said, 'I feel so dumb about this.'

[FAIL]

Cambodian radio presenter Chiang Goan fell 100 feet from a tower and survived, putting his good fortune down to the lucky goat charm he wore round his neck. Wishing to prove the power of the charm with his listeners, Goan invited a soldier down to the radio station and asked him to fire a bullet at him. Goan died instantly.

Out-of-work 41-year-old actor Luther Charles was desperate for a part. When he saw an advertisement in 1995 for a musical at the Ohio Theatre, which required 'Genuine earless performers', he did what anyone in his situation would; after drinking a bottle of whiskey and numbing them with ice, he cut off his ears. He turned up at the auditions, stunning the show's producers. They explained that the ad had been a misprint; it should have said 'fearless' performers. Charles failed to get the part and instead was referred for psychiatric treatment.

FAIL

Jerry Stromyer, a 24-year-old man from Kincaid, West Virginia, watched as one of the guests at a party tried to detonate a blasting cap by putting it in an aquarium and connecting it to a battery. When it failed to explode he grabbed the cap and tried a method of his own. According to Corporal Payne of the Kincaid Police Department, 'He put it in his mouth and bit down. It blew all his teeth off, his tongue and his lips.'

A spokesman for the Charleston Area Medical Division said, 'I just can't imagine anyone doing something like that.'

No one will ever know why 55-year-old Tony Perner decided to stand in the middle of the runway of an airstrip in East Moriches, New York, drop his trousers and moon the pilot of a light aircraft taking off. The pilot, Frederick Spadaro, hit Mr Perner, critically injuring him. He told police that he didn't see the victim as it was dark.

FAIL

Stephen Stills was a 36-year-old town alderman in Gentry, Arkansas, who should have known better when he decided to shoot cans and bottles off a friend's head with a .22-calibre rifle. Although the targets were less than 20 feet away he still managed to miss and was charged with murder.

Toronto lawyer Garry Hoy was demonstrating the strength of his office window in the Dominion Bank Tower to a bunch of visiting law students. He'd done this many times before – except this time, when he shoulder-charged the glass, it broke and he plunged 24 floors to his death.

Professional hypnotist Filadelfio Munafo thought he had the situation under control when two armed men broke into his office in Milan. He put them into a trance and ordered them to hand over their guns. As he was in the process of hypnotizing the men one of them shot him. Munafo later said, 'I was sure I had them in my power.'

[FAIL]

Bungee jumper William Brotherton was better at jumping than maths. In his last jump he leaped out of a tethered hot-air balloon over a field in Arvada, Colorado, only to discover that he'd made the cord 70 feet too long.

To celebrate the opening of Bristol Science Museum in March 1991, it was visited by a delegation of Mensa members led by their group's international president. Billed by the local paper as '25 of the brainiest people in the world', none of the Mensa members could find the museum, which was located right next to the railway station.

They were eventually located by a member of the museum staff down a side street, wandering around 'like a bunch of lost sheep'.

[FAIL]

In 1969, Hurricane Camille reached the Mississippi Gulf Coast, causing hundreds of thousands of dollars of damage and the loss of 143 lives. Many of the casualties had been caught by surprise and were unable to escape the storm. However, 20 of its victims were killed when they decided to stay and hold a beachfront 'hurricane party'. Despite pleas to evacuate by authorities, the barbecue was in full swing on the terrace of a second-floor apartment; the partygoers were convinced that being above ground level meant they would be safe – until a 24-foot wave destroyed the building and most of those left in it.

Kerry Bingham had been out drinking with his friends in Tacoma, Washington State, when bungee jumping became a hot topic of conversation. Soon Kerry and nine other men trooped out of the pub and along to the Tacoma Narrows Bridge, all determined to perform their first bungee jump. The absence of any bungee rope did not deter them, as ringleader Kerry decided that a coil of electric cable lying nearby would be just fine.

Tying one end to the bridge and one end around his ankle Kerry leaped off the side. According to witnesses he fell about 40 feet before the cable tightened, yanking off his foot at the ankle. He was rescued from the icy waters by two fishermen.

FAIL

Police in Toronto, Canada, didn't have far to go to arrest a man for drink driving after he crashed into one of their patrol cars parked directly outside their police station. The only excuse the 60-year-old driver could offer was that he was checking whether he was sober enough to drive.

When Mark Twain saw his obituary in the *New York Journal* of 1 June 1897, he is said to have commented, 'Reports of my death have been greatly exaggerated.'

However, 24-year-old Armando Cassa from Puerto Rico had a more tragic reaction when he heard reports that he'd died in a fire. Rather than utter a witty quip like Twain he threw himself off the top of his high-rise apartment block.

BEASTLY BLUNDERS

> **'Ambition is the last refuge of the failure.'**
> OSCAR WILDE

***Four legs good, two legs bad? When you consider how
some people interact with creatures great and small,
in many cases it's not the animals that are dumb...***

Iranian Ali-Asghar Ahani was hunting for snakes in 1990 when
he came across a prize specimen, trapping the creature
helplessly on the ground by pressing his rifle butt behind its
head. Assuming the gun was another predator attacking it, the
snake coiled its body around the barrel, accidentally pulling the
trigger and killing Mr Ahani in front of a fellow hunter.

FAIL

No one really knows why Ronald Demuth from Vermont
decided to demonstrate the adhesive power of Crazy Glue, a
super-strong epoxy compound, by coating his hands with it
and then placing them on a rhino's buttocks in a petting zoo.
The surreal event took place at the Eagle's Rock African Safari

Zoo. The rhino, Sally, was quite tame so she wasn't scared, but as it dawned on her that the man was firmly attached to her backside, she panicked and began charging around her compound. To add insult to injury, she had been feeling unwell so her keeper had given her a strong laxative. During the stampede the laxative began to work and it wasn't long before Ronald, still being pulled along behind Sally, was showered with 30 gallons of liquid rhino dung.

Sally was eventually sedated and a solvent was used to remove Ronald's hands from her buttocks. After he was taken away to be cleaned up the zoo caretaker made a comment others might consider as 'stating the obvious': 'I don't think he'll be playing with Crazy Glue for a while.'

FAIL

The Times of 19 October 1986 carried the story of Emilio Tarra, a crewmember of the 1986 America's Cup race, who was driving from Perth towards Adelaide during the Australian leg of the race. En route, his car sideswiped a kangaroo, leaving it sprawled across the road.

Tarra got out of his car and, assuming the kangaroo was dead, decided to take a novelty photograph to show his colleagues. Dressing the kangaroo up in his smart team blazer he propped it against his car to take its photograph. As he was focusing his camera the kangaroo, which had only been stunned, woke up and bounded back off into the bush – taking with it the jacket, which contained Tarra's passport, $2,000 (£1,250) worth of cash and his credit cards.

British ornithologist Phillip Ball was determined to see the rufous fishing owl, one of the rarest owls in existence and found in West Africa. After hearing of an example being sighted in the Edo region of Nigeria, Phillip travelled to the country and organized an expedition to locate the bird. The tribe with which he was travelling laid on a sumptuous feast for their visitor. Tucking in, Phillip enquired what was in the stew he was eating. It was a rufous fishing owl.

The next day he took some photos of local wildlife and went home.

[FAIL]

An ice-cream van driver in Los Angeles had parked to make a delivery when, without warning, a goat jumped through the open doorway into the cab and accidentally released the handbrake. The van careered down a hill before crashing into a tree, scattering produce everywhere. According to a witness, the goat jumped from the cab, helped himself to an ice cream, then trotted off, none the worse for his ordeal.

An Alsatian police dog named Remus was involved in tracking down an armed robber when the police accompanying him saw their suspect. Remus's handler let him off his leash with the command, 'Get him!'

Remus obliged but the man he viciously pinned to the ground was Inspector David Cox of the Leicester police – the man leading the chase.

[FAIL]

A barbed warbler landed in South Woodham Ferrers, Essex, in December 1992, when it should have been enjoying the warm Kenyan weather. Word got round and soon birdwatchers from all over Britain descended on the area just to catch a sight of it. They watched, delighted, as the bird hopped around right in front of them – then the unspeakable happened. An unknown black cat that had been seen stalking around the area pounced, and ran off with the poor barbed warbler in its mouth.

A Siamese cat called Missy innocently strolled across her owner's computer keyboard at her home in Los Angeles – and accidentally hacked into a bank. By coincidence, the cat's steps had tapped out a special five-letter code sequence and erased $50,000 (£31,000) from customer accounts. The bank later promised to upgrade its security.

Percy the racing pigeon set off from Folkestone in Kent in 1992, setting out for home in Billingham, Cleveland. Instead, he ended up in Shanghai, China, 6,000 miles off course!

Percy's owner, George Gamble, gave him up for lost. Five years passed and, in March 1997, George was stunned to get a phone call from a Chinese woman who had identified Percy through the code attached to his leg. He was alive and well and, George thought, probably too ashamed to come home.

Snake charmer Shahidul Islam from Bangladesh was travelling on a bus that plunged off a road. His snakes escaped in the accident and prevented rescuers reaching the charmer, who later died from his injuries.

FAIL

In the 1960s the CIA is said to have spent over $20 million (£12.49 million) on a project that used cats as recording devices. Microphones, antennae and batteries were surgically implanted into cats that were then set loose near the Russian embassy. The idea was that an innocent-looking cat would be able to walk right up to groups of communist officials and eavesdrop on their conversation, transmitting it back to US agents. The first cat sent into the field was run over by a taxi when it was let loose, and operation 'Acoustic Kitty' was abandoned shortly thereafter.

Neil Simmons was a keen birdwatcher and was amazed when one of his many attempts to mimic the distinctive hoot of the tawny owls in his garden was met with a response. Every night in 1996 he would 'to-whit, to-whoo' and receive a corresponding 'to-whit, to-whoo' in response.

He was very disappointed to discover that the hoots were not from an owl but from the lips of his neighbour, Fred Cornes, who was also acting under the misapprehension that his own attempts at mimicking the owls were working.

☹

In February 1991 about 50 onlookers and police watched as a vet and game warden attempted to rescue a black bear that had climbed a pine tree in Keithville, Louisiana. Tranquillizing darts were fired at the creature with nets strung between the trees to catch it.

The darts seemed to do the trick. The bear, which had been quite active, instantly calmed down but still refused to drop to the ground. Then, to the surprise of the crowd, it suddenly became agitated and began moving violently.

Rather than fire more darts a decision was made to cut the tree down and rescue the bear that way. Foresters were called and carefully cut the tree and lowered it to the ground – where they were then able to remove the large black plastic bin bag caught in the branches.

FAIL

A Mr Gordon was driving in Darwin, Australia, when he and a friend saw a king brown, one of the most venomous snakes in the world. Drunk at the time, Gordon decided to pick the snake up. The consequence was predictable: the snake bit his hand. Throwing the snake into a plastic bag Gordon's friend sped off to the nearest hospital so they could administer an antidote. During the journey however, Gordon couldn't resist checking up on the snake so he put his hand back in the bag. The snake then bit him eight more times. As a result of the additional venom Gordon lost an arm and the use of his legs.

An act of what might be interpreted as fish revenge took place in July 1996. Brazilian fisherman Nathon do Nascimento was waiting for fish to bite in the Maguari River. It was a hot, lazy day and Nascimento couldn't help but let out a long, intense yawn. It was at this exact time that a six-inch-long fish leaped clean out of the water and lodged itself in the fisherman's throat.

Unable to breathe, Nascimento thrashed about, attracting the attention of two other fishermen. They were unable to reach the fish, which had by now got itself wedged even further down his throat, suffocating its human victim.

CRIME DOESN'T PAY

> *'I think you can have 10,000 explanations for failure,
> but no good explanation for success.'*
>
> PAULO COELHO

*You've heard all about daring criminal masterminds.
Well, you won't find any in this particular chapter...*

FAIL

In February 1979, six Peruvian gunmen used a light aircraft to rob an isolated farm in the mountainous north of the country, escaping with the equivalent of £500. Unfortunately it had cost them considerably more than this to hire and fuel the aircraft.

Texan Kim Molito was convicted of a burglary in San Antonio in 1992 and told he would face seven years behind bars. He protested against the length of his sentence, arguing that seven was his unlucky number. The judge sympathized and changed the sentence to eight years.

In 1990 bank robber Danny Simpson of Ottawa, Canada, was given a six-year prison sentence for robbing a bank of $6,000 (£3,750) using an old Colt .45 pistol. After the gun was impounded by the police, it was identified as being a very rare collector's item, one of only 100 made under licence by the Ross Rifle Company in Quebec during the First World War. In fact, its value was estimated as at least $12,000 (£7,500), which meant if Simpson had simply sold the pistol instead of using it to rob the bank, he would have got twice what he had stolen.

Robbers who took part in a £175,000 raid on a jeweller's at a shopping centre near Rainham in Kent in December 2008 hired a getaway driver with a difference: he had no arms. Despite his disability, 18-year-old John Smith managed to lead the police on a terrifying 30-mile chase reaching speeds of up to 100 m.p.h., with other gang members changing gear for him. The gang was eventually caught when police forced their car into a wall. Smith wasn't wearing his prosthetic arms at the time of the getaway and it's not known why the robbers thought he was the best man for the job.

[FAIL]

In August 1995 a man broke into a woman's house in Kuala Lumpur. To keep her quiet while he stole her property he tried to force her to down a drugged drink. The hysterical woman thought it was poison and refused to drink it, so the would-be thief took a gulp to prove it was quite safe. He promptly collapsed and was later arrested.

A gang broke into the Southern Leisure Centre in Chichester and attempted to steal the safe using sophisticated cutting equipment. They abandoned their mission after they had managed to weld the safe door completely shut.

In November 1993 Sergio de Sa, a Brazilian glue sniffer, broke into a glue factory. After trying out various solvents he eventually found a vat of his favourite glue being processed and immediately started inhaling. Overcome by fumes he passed out and as he fell to the ground, pulled the whole vat over.

By the time de Sa regained consciousness he was stuck fast to the factory floor where he remained until staff arrived the next morning, followed shortly by the police, who arrested him.

[FAIL]

In February 1990 a would-be thief chose a completely inappropriate target for his robbery – a firearms shop in Renton, Seattle, Washington, that was full of customers. As if a shop full of gun-carrying members of the public wasn't bad enough, a uniformed King County policeman was also present, chatting to the staff. Even this didn't dissuade the robber from calmly firing his gun in the air and announcing that a hold-up was in progress. He was immediately shot dead by the cop and a sales assistant.

In January 1997 Michael Coulter stole trainers, socks and boxer shorts from a shop in Cookstown, County Tyrone. He was immediately identified by staff, who recognized him: at seven feet five inches tall, he was Ireland's tallest man.

A drunk thief who tried to hold up a garage in Ionia, Michigan, wasn't the brightest button in the box. After the staff refused to hand over their takings he threatened to call the police. After they refused a second time he did call the police. He was arrested.

The wannabe robber who tried to hold up Mohammed Razaq's convenience store in Wandsworth, London, in July 1979 underestimated one thing: Mr Razaq's powers of observation. After the intruder demanded the contents of the till or he'd shoot, a cool Mr Razaq calmly pointed out that the thief wasn't actually holding a gun.

The thief admitted that he wasn't, but added that if the shop owner was going to be difficult, he could go home and get one. With that, he left the shop and was never seen again.

In January 2007 Kurt Husfeldt successfully managed to steal a consignment of sophisticated-looking mobile phones from a warehouse in Lindenhurst, New York, but was astonished when police turned up on his doorstep minutes after he reached home. It turned out they weren't phones at all, but Global Positioning Systems designed to help the authorities locate snowploughs lost in drifts. They'd tracked him as soon as he switched one on.

[FAIL]

It had taken many months of careful planning but soon the small-time criminal was ready to carry out his daring robbery. Brandishing a pistol he walked into a bank in Columbia, Tennessee, yelling, 'Give me your money!' He was met with a wall of puzzled silence from the employees. Later he discovered that the bank had closed down a while ago and the building was now the offices of an insurance company.

Three Miami teenagers who attempted to rob a local grocery store ended up shooting each other in the process. In February 1996 Wesley Steny, Jeanis Caty and an unnamed accomplice walked into a mini-mart and demanded that the checkout staff open the cash registers then hit the floor.

Caty leaned across the counter to reach the money in the till and in the process accidentally shot Steny in his thigh. Falling to the floor in pain, Steny accidentally fired his own gun, managing somehow to hit Caty in both his hands and his leg.

The third, unharmed, robber grabbed $200 (£125) before the gang limped out of the store. Police followed the blood trail to a local hospital where the suspects were promptly arrested.

In November 1996 a would-be thief entered the Burger King in Ypsilanti, Michigan, pointed a gun at the staff and demanded money. He was politely informed that the tills couldn't be opened without a food order being placed. The man demanded the cheapest thing on the menu, onion rings, only to be told that they weren't available for breakfast.

Frustrated, he stormed out empty-handed.

Pursued by police after a failed robbery in Connecticut in 1997, a would-be thief known only as Maurice drove into the parking lot of a shopping mall, abandoned his car and ran into the main entrance. To his surprise he found himself trapped between doors that automatically locked in front and behind him. The shopping mall was actually the MacDougall Correctional Institution, a high-security state prison.

FAIL

Javier Ortiz, aged 25, of Badajoz, Spain, robbed a bank and for reasons not entirely clear, thought the best way to avoid capture would be to hide in a nearby convent. He managed to get in undetected and steal a nun's habit, but hunger got the better of him so he found his way into the kitchen and stole a leg of ham.

Hearing footsteps, Ortiz decided to hide the ham down his habit, conceal his face and act nonchalantly. The footsteps he heard belonged to the Mother Superior, who was fairly sure she didn't have any pregnant nuns in the convent and called the police.

Would-be bank robber Steven King tried to rob a bank in the town of Merced, California, threatening staff discreetly by making the shape of a gun with his thumb and forefinger, so as not to alert security. Unfortunately he forgot to keep his hand inside his trouser pocket and was arrested by guards.

Clive Castro of Cooperville, Texas, robbed a bank, ran out as fast as he could and yanked open the door of the first car he saw in the slow-moving traffic outside with the aim of commandeering it and driving himself to safety. Unfortunately the car he chose was an unmarked police car.

FAIL

Cash-strapped Frederick Field had an ingenious idea for making money: confessing to a murder knowing full well there was no way he could be convicted for a crime he didn't commit, then selling his story to the press about how he'd been persecuted. He tried it in 1931 and received a fortune from the *News of the World*. Down on his luck five years later, he noticed a story in the press about the death of a rich widow, Beatrice Sutton – and he confessed to her murder. This time, though, the jury believed him and found him guilty. Field was hanged later that year.

POLITICIANS SAY THE STUPIDEST THINGS

> *'In politics, stupidity is not a handicap.'*
> NAPOLEON BONAPARTE

There's one thing you can definitely trust politicians to do: make a fool of themselves. Put them in front of a microphone and they'll always make the most inappropriate, brainless and ill-judged statements in public...

'The internet is a great way to get on the net.'
BOB DOLE, REPUBLICAN PRESIDENTIAL CANDIDATE

[FAIL]

'For NASA, space is still a high priority.'
DAN QUAYLE, FORMER US VICE-PRESIDENT

'Queen Elizabeth Taylor...'

THAI PRIME MINISTER BANHARN SILPA-ARCHA,
REFERRING TO THE QUEEN OF ENGLAND DURING
HER 1996 STATE VISIT

'Traditionally, most of Australia's imports come
from overseas.'

KEPPEL ENDERBERY, FORMER AUSTRALIAN
CABINET MINISTER

'The Holocaust was an obscene period in our nation's history. I mean in this century's history. But we all lived in this century. I didn't live in this century.'

DAN QUAYLE, FORMER US VICE-PRESIDENT

'If I find out who is the maker of the nine seasons of *The Octopus* and who has written books on the Mafia, which give such a bad image to Italy across the world, I swear that I will strangle them.'

FORMER ITALIAN PRIME MINISTER SILVIO BERLUSCONI ON THE ITALIAN TV SERIES ABOUT THE MAFIA

FAIL

'China is a big country, inhabited by many Chinese.'

CHARLES DE GAULLE, FORMER FRENCH PRESIDENT

'It isn't pollution that's harming our environment. It's the impurities in our air and water that are doing it.'

DAN QUAYLE, FORMER US VICE-PRESIDENT

FAIL

'All the waste in a year from a nuclear power plant can be stored under a desk.'

RONALD REAGAN, FORMER US PRESIDENT (IN REALITY THE AVERAGE NUCLEAR POWER PLANT GENERATES 30 TONS OF RADIOACTIVE WASTE EVERY YEAR)

'How can one be fascinated by those fights of obese guys with Brylcreemed buns? Sumo is not an intellectual's sport!'

NICOLAS SARKOZY, FORMER FRENCH PRESIDENT –
EVER THE DIPLOMAT

'I don't understand how they can call me anti-Latino when I've made four movies in Mexico.'

ARNOLD SCHWARZENEGGER, FORMER GOVERNOR OF CALIFORNIA

'I do not like this word "bomb". It is not a bomb. It is a device that is exploding.'

JACQUES LE BLANC, FRENCH AMBASSADOR,
ON NUCLEAR WEAPONS

David Lloyd George, former British prime minister, didn't have a great deal of political insight. In 1934 he declared, 'Believe me, Germany is unable to wage war.' Two years later he was absolutely convinced that 'Germany has no desire to attack any country in Europe'.

FAIL

President Woodrow Wilson also wasn't a very good judge on wars and their impact. In January 1917, two months before the US entered the First World War, he stated, 'There will be no war.' In January 1918 he predicted that the First World War would be the last great global conflict, calling it, 'The culmination and final war for human liberty.'

'Why can't these Arabs and Jews resolve their differences at the conference table like good Christians?'

WARREN AUSTIN, US AMBASSADOR TO THE UNITED NATIONS,
DURING THE 1948 ISRAELI WAR OF INDEPENDENCE

[**FAIL**]

In 1948 a Washington DC radio station asked various foreign ambassadors what they would like most for Christmas. The French ambassador said, 'Peace throughout the world.' The Russian ambassador commented, 'Freedom for all people enslaved by imperialism.' The British ambassador, Sir Oliver Franks, said, 'Well, it's very kind of you to ask. I'd quite like a box of crystallized fruit.'

At a large government reception in December 1975 US President Gerald Ford toasted the health of 'the president of Israel'. That would have been fine – except the reception was for Anwar Sadat, the leader of Egypt.

[**FAIL**]

'You must obey the law, always, not only when they grab you by your special place.'

VLADIMIR PUTIN, FORMER RUSSIAN PREMIER, DISPLAYING HIS
TOUCHY-FEELY TYPE OF GOVERNMENT

'This is a great day for France!'

PRESIDENT RICHARD NIXON AT FRENCH PRESIDENT
CHARLES DE GAULLE'S FUNERAL

'I've now been in 57 states – I think one left to go.'

BARACK OBAMA AT A PRESIDENTIAL CAMPAIGN EVENT
IN BEAVERTON, OREGON, 2008

'I think that gay marriage should be between
a man and a woman.'

ARNOLD SCHWARZENEGGER,
FORMER GOVERNOR OF CALIFORNIA

'We are not without accomplishment.
We have managed to distribute poverty equally.'

NGUYEN CO THACH, VIETNAMESE FOREIGN MINISTER

'I think incest can be handled as a family matter
within the family.'

JAY DICKEY, JR, US REPRESENTATIVE FROM ARKANSAS

'All of 'em, any of 'em that have been in front of me
over all these years.'

FORMER REPUBLICAN PARTY VICE-PRESIDENTIAL NOMINEE
SARAH PALIN, WHEN ASKED TO NAME ANY NEWSPAPER OR
MAGAZINE THAT SHE READS

George W. Bush might have been the 43rd president of the United States but he was the number-one world leader when it came to saying the stupidest things:

- 'That's a chapter, the last chapter of the twentieth, twentieth, twenty-first century that most of us would rather forget. The last chapter of the twentieth century. This is the first chapter of the twenty-first century.'

- 'Well, I think if you say you're going to do something and don't do it, that's trustworthiness.'

- 'Families is where our nation finds hope, where wings take dream.'

- 'Rarely is the question asked: is our children learning?'

- 'It's clearly a budget. It's got a lot of numbers in it.'

- 'I think we agree: the past is over.'

- 'Our enemies are innovative and resourceful, and so are we. They never stop thinking about new ways to harm our country and our people, and neither do we.'

- On his Community Service Initiative: 'And so, in my state of the ... my state of the Union ... or state ... my speech to the nation, whatever you want to call it, speech to the nation ... I asked Americans to give 4,000 years ... 4,000 hours over the next ... the rest of your life ... of service to America.'

- On the war against terrorism: 'And there is no doubt in my mind, not one doubt in my mind, that we will fail.'

- 'I have opinions of my own – strong opinions – but I don't always agree with them.'

FAIL

BUREAUCRATIC BALLS-UPS

It has been said that the best way to deal with bureaucracy is to smile and act stupid. The problem is, that's what most bureaucrats do...

☹

On 4 January 1971, George Mellendorf, a soldier serving in Vietnam, sent a letter to President Nixon complaining about how long the mail took to reach them. Seven years later, in February 1978, the US Post Office delivered the letter to the former President Nixon at his home address in San Clemente, California.

[FAIL]

Britain's National Health Service swung into action to help a tourist who collapsed while on a tour of Buckingham Palace in 1992. After being treated he was quickly repatriated and awoke to find himself in Santiago, Chile. The only problem was that he came from Santiago in Spain – 700 miles away rather than 7,000.

The US Postal Service was proud of its 1993 'Legends of the West' stamp series, which included a photo of the Afro-American rodeo star Bill Pickett, who was credited with inventing steer-wrestling. Bill's descendants should have been proud too, but they weren't: the stamps actually featured Bill's brother, Ben. The Postal Service was forced to withdraw all five million stamps from every single post office at a cost of over $1 million (£625,000).

Six years later it printed a stamp depicting the Grand Canyon; the caption placed it in Colorado rather than Arizona.

[FAIL]

In September 1993, after investigating ways to make the government far more efficient, Vice-president Al Gore released a 168-page report titled, *Creating a Government That Works Better and Costs Less* at a cost of $4 (£2.50) per copy. An internal report later stated that had the report not been produced on the most expensive Grade 1 coated high-gloss paper on a rush schedule over the Labor Day weekend, it could have cost just 90 cents (56 pence) a copy.

In January 1991 Chuck Barr of Jamestown, California, received a fine from his local library for an overdue book. He queried the amount due, feeling that it was a bit excessive: the fine was for $40,000,000,000,000 – or 40 trillion dollars (25 trillion pounds), almost seven times more than the US national debt. The fine was waived.

A witness who was sworn in at a Syracuse, New York, courthouse had to re-take her oath after a court official realized that instead of swearing on the Bible, she had in fact used an inappropriate book that was on the courthouse table by mistake – a Danielle Steele romance.

There was a mix-up in the photo library when the Australian railway system launched a campaign in January 1988 against fare-dodgers. The picture of the would-be criminal shown approaching the barriers at Calvary station was actually the town's mayor.

Members of an Atlantic City, New Jersey, council passed a resolution twinning their city with Bucharest, Hungary. Unfortunately for them, Bucharest is in Romania.

[FAIL]

The Tennessee Valley Authority, a government-owned energy company, received 46 suggestions from staff that saved the company $580,000 (£362,200). The cost of administering the programme and rewarding employees for their suggestions was $700,000 (£437,100).

When Railtrack published its *Great Britain Railway Passenger Timetable* in 1995, the 2,100-page document was riddled with so many errors that a separate 57-page supplement was issued to correct it. The story didn't end there, however. When it was discovered that the corrections were incorrect, a third document of 246 pages had to be issued to amend it.

[FAIL]

Solihull Council hired a firm of contractors to demolish some old farm buildings on the Stratford Road near Birmingham in December 1980. Not blessed with a keen sense of direction, the contractor took a wrong turning and headed for the building opposite. This was Monkspath Hall, a beautiful listed building that dated back to 1775 and one of the most historic, well-preserved farmhouses in the Midlands. It was a Sunday morning so there were few people to witness – and possibly prevent – the demolition of Monkspath Hall in just 45 minutes.

The local government in Transylvania, Romania, received so many complaints about lazy road workers leaning on their shovels and resting when they should have been working that they hit upon an ingenious idea: shorten the handles.

Mayor Gheorghe Funar commented that this improvement meant that the handles 'can no longer be used as a leaning point by those who meditate while at work'.

It wasn't long, however, before the labourers discovered that their new shovels weren't as bad as they had first thought. It was true they couldn't lean against them – but they could still take it easy. The new shovels were the perfect height for sitting on.

Canada's federal flight regulations made it an offence to enter an aircraft when it was in flight.

In 1986 the UK Post Office launched a promotion to get people to remember their postcode. This took the form of a competition called 'What's Your Postcode?' Unfortunately the Post Office's own postcode on the entry form was incorrect. They blamed it on a 'printing error'.

The Long Island Lighting Company in New York informed the US Nuclear Regulatory Commission that in the unlikely event of a nuclear accident at the Shoreham Power Plant residents would all be evacuated to the Nassau Coliseum – unless a ball game was in progress at the time.

Taiwan's Council for Agricultural Planning and Development commissioned a comprehensive study into eating habits. This came to two startling conclusions: that people eat lunch because they are hungry, and that lunch is often one of the three meals a day.

In 1976, under the directive of the EEC (as it was then known), the Irish government was forced to introduce equal-opportunities legislation to make sure there was equal pay between the sexes. The Dublin government advertised for an Equal Pay Enforcement Officer to make sure the policy was being imposed – offering different pay scales for men and women.

[FAIL]

Assistant District Attorney Paul Hermann happened to look up at the Potter County courthouse in Texas and wondered why the flag of Chile was flying over it. On investigation it was discovered that the new flag that had recently been delivered had been marked 'Texas' and no one had even noticed the mistake.

Thanks to the incompetence of Pennsylvanian health officials, Catherine Yasinchuk spent 48 years in a mental institution. In 1921 police found a tearful young girl walking the city's streets and assumed her hysterical babbling was a sign of mental illness. She was committed to Philadelphia State Hospital, but it was only in 1968 that a new director recognized that the 'tongues' Yasinchuk was speaking in were actually just Ukrainian – the only language she could speak.

The great Ecuadorian poet and patriot José Joaquín de Olmedo was twice mayor of the city of Guayaquil, so it was understandable that when he died in 1847 the city fathers would erect a statue in his honour. Unfortunately, the treasury didn't have enough funds for a sculptor, so the city did the next best thing: they bought a statue of the English poet Lord Byron from a London junk dealer and changed the plaque to Olmedo's name.

Residents of Easingwold, near York, were pleased to see a new postbox appear attached to the side of a pole in their town. Delight soon turned to disgust, however, when they discovered it wasn't actually a postbox, but rather a depository for doggie-do. The bin should have been green but had been painted red in error, causing the confusion.

FAIL

In the summer of 1986 the East Essex Health Authority launched a 'Better Health' campaign using an expensively commissioned logo showing a cardiogram. It was just before the campaign went public that someone realized that the cardiogram actually showed the patient had died.

No one could figure out why a huge safe-sex campaign orchestrated by the Society for Family Health in Johannesburg in February 1999 actually resulted in an *increase* in sexually transmitted diseases and unwanted pregnancies. Then it was discovered that the free condoms that had been distributed were stapled to an educational pamphlet – right through their centres.

BUSINESS BUNGLES

> *'Failure doesn't mean you're a failure. It just means you haven't succeeded yet.'*
>
> ROBERT H. SCHULLER

It's said that success in most businesses and corporations depends more on energy and drive than it does on intelligence. This explains why some decisions made within them can be so dumb...

☹

While *E.T.* was in pre-production, Steven Spielberg's Amblin Entertainment approached Mars for permission for Elliott to lay a trail of M&Ms to lure the extraterrestrial. Mars declined, apparently not wanting its product associated with an alien, so Spielberg then approached the Hershey Company, which gladly gave him permission to feature its rival candy, Reese's Pieces. The film became a massive worldwide hit in 1982 and sales of Reese's Pieces overtook M&Ms for the first time.

[FAIL]

Whoever named Emu Airways of Australia was correct in knowing that it was a native bird of the country. What they might not have considered was that the emu is totally incapable of flight.

⊗

In April 1991, Gerald Ratner, owner of the high-street jewellers that bore his name, was giving a talk at the Institute of Directors about his business. He commented, 'We also do cut-glass Sherry decanters complete with six glasses on a silver-plated tray, all for £4.95. People say, "How can you sell this for such a low price?" I say, "Because it's total crap."' He added that Ratners' earrings were 'Cheaper than an M&S prawn sandwich but probably wouldn't last as long.'

Journalists invited to his speech reported these comments and, within days, his company had dropped £500 million in value. Ratner was later sacked and the name, by then synonymous with 'crap', disappeared from the high streets.

FAIL

In 1849 Brooklyn, New York, inventor Walter Hunt invented and patented the safety pin and then sold all the rights for $400 (£250). A hundred years later the US was producing an estimated five billion safety pins a year. Hunt died penniless in 1859.

Silo was an electronics retailer and discounter that operated throughout the United States until its demise in 1995. To highlight its low prices in 1986 it ran a television commercial stating that it was selling stereo systems for '299 bananas' – thinking that everyone knew that bananas meant dollars. It turns out they didn't, and customers started turning up with

299 bananas (costing about $40/£25) to exchange for a brand-new stereo. The company honoured the price in order to maintain the goodwill of its shoppers, losing over $10,000 (£6,245) in one day – but immediately pulled the ads before word spread and more customers turned up with wheelbarrows full of fruit.

[FAIL]

An unnamed British bank decided to mail 2,000 of its wealthiest customers in 1993 to promote a range of exclusive financial services. So important were these clients that the mail-merge programme was first tested using a fictitious name. Unfortunately due to human error the fake name ended up being used for everyone; recipients received letters addressed: 'Dear Rich Bastard'.

Despite millions being spent on R&D and focus groups, some shoe companies still fail to get it right when it comes to naming products.

To commemorate St Patrick's Day in 2012, Nike introduced its range of 'Black and Tan' sneakers as a reference to Ireland's greatest export, Guinness. The beer-themed trainer had a black-leather upper with tan elements, a creamy swoosh and an image of a pint inside. What Nike failed to appreciate was that the Black and Tans was the name of the brutal British paramilitary unit during the 1920s Irish Independence Wars. One critic said that naming the trainer Black and Tan was comparable to calling it al-Qaeda. Nike apologized for its insensitivity.

This wasn't the first time Nike has insulted a large group of people. In 1997 Muslims were understandably upset when the 'flaming air' logo for Nike Air sneakers resembled the Arabic form of God's name, 'Allah'. In response to the outcry Nike pulled more than 38,000 pairs of sneakers from the market.

Other misjudged trainer names include the 1995 Incubus trainer from Reebok – a product that shared its name with a demon that sexually assaulted women. Reebok had to issue stickers to cover up the product name on over 50,000 boxes.

Not to be outdone, in 1999 Umbro came under fire after launching the Zyklon trainer, which shared its name with the gas used in Nazi extermination chambers. Umbro apologized and a spokesperson said, 'I think in future we will be checking the names we use more carefully.'

[FAIL]

In 1984 international courier company FedEx introduced a service called Zapmail. A company could bring a document to a FedEx office where it would be faxed to another FedEx office in the destination city. The document would then be printed out and delivered by a courier to the addressee – avoiding the need for costly and time-consuming cross-country transportation. By the time the service was up and running, fax machines suddenly became affordable and every business had one. After losing more than $200 million, (£125 million) Zapmail was discontinued in 1986.

In November 1980 Texaco began drilling for oil in the middle of the 1,100-acre Lake Peigneur in Louisiana. It managed to drill into an old salt mine beneath the lake, which then filled with water. The ensuing whirlpool sucked down the drilling rig, eight tugboats, nine barges and 65 acres of surrounding terrain.

The broadcaster Carlton TV had to refund British Airways the cost of its advertising space when in 1993 it accidentally ran one of the airline's commercials during a break in the aircraft disaster movie, *Terror in the Sky*.

The first oil to be discovered in America was found by farmers in Pennsylvania. Some sold it as a medicinal cure for gout and fallen arches. Less-enterprising farmers, dismayed that their water supply contained 'black glue', sold off their land for a pittance and moved away.

FAIL

Advertising giant Saatchi and Saatchi thought it had hit it big when its New Zealand office devised what it called the 'Auckland Big A' campaign. The idea was to create pride in the city by encouraging residents to greet each other by making a large 'A' symbol, touching the tips of their thumbs and forefingers together. It seemed like a good idea at the time but the plan was soon abandoned when the Deaf Association of New Zealand pointed out that the hand gesture was also the internationally recognized sign for vagina.

MGM boss Louis B. Mayer turned down Mickey Mouse in 1927, telling a young Walt Disney that it would never catch on and that pregnant women would be frightened when they saw a giant mouse on the screen. After this rejection, Walt and his brother Roy decided to make and distribute Mickey Mouse movies on their own. In 2011 Disney employed 156,000 people worldwide with revenues of nearly $41 billion (£25.6 billion).

FAIL

A Hitler-themed restaurant was probably not his best business decision, but that's what Indian businessman Punit Shablok decided would set his venture apart. The grand opening of Hitler's Cross took place on 18 August 2006; diners could enjoy a good meal surrounded by photos of Hitler, Nazi propaganda posters and huge Swastika flags.

Admitting that he wasn't that familiar with western history, Mr Shablok said he wanted a name with an authentic European ring to it. The German consul-general politely suggested that he might want to consider 'something less controversial'.

A Canberra-based confectioner underestimated the offence his new Easter chocolate line would cause. As its name suggests, his 'Sweet Jesus' was a chocolate Messiah on a cross. When you bit into him, red jelly oozed out. The company commented, 'The object is to put religion back into Easter with an edible icon.'

FAIL

The grandfather of film star Lana Turner owned a half-share in a new company that had started bottling a fizzy drink. He thought the drink's name would affect its saleability and wanted to change it – without success. In frustration he sold his 50 per cent share. It's a pity, because Coca-Cola really caught on…

On three separate occasions from 1922–23, Coca-Cola had the chance to buy its rival, the Pepsi-Cola Company, for a bargain $1,000 (£625). The company turned it down each time, missing the opportunity to take over what would become its arch-rival.

McDonald's launched its 'When the US Wins, You Win' promotion to link in with the 1984 Olympics in Los Angeles where the company offered free Big Macs, fries and Coke for every medal the US Olympic team won. What they couldn't have predicted was that in retaliation for the US boycott of the 1980 Games as a protest against the Soviet invasion of Afghanistan, the Russians and East Germans stayed away from the 1984 Olympics. Without their most serious competition, Team USA won many more events than they anticipated. The promotion was a disaster for McDonald's and cost it millions.

FAIL

In 1938, Joe Schuster and Jerry Siegel sold all rights to a comic book character they'd invented, agreeing a fee of just $65 each from their publisher.

The character's name? Superman.

MILITARY MISTAKES

> *'If at first you don't succeed, destroy all evidence that you tried.'*
>
> STEVEN WRIGHT

There's a saying in the armed forces that there's the right way, the wrong way and the military way. Unfortunately, in most cases the military way is also the wrong way...

[FAIL]

To reduce the possibility of contracting typhoid during an epidemic, the US Army once issued this sage advice: 'All ice cubes will be boiled before using.'

In 1993 a very suspicious-looking package was found outside the Territorial Army centre in Bristol. The police were called, who then alerted an army bomb-disposal team. In a controlled explosion, the package was destroyed. It was then found to contain leaflets on how to identify suspicious-looking packages.

During the 1990–91 Gulf War the Iraqi propaganda machine created 'Baghdad Betty', a character whose radio broadcasts were designed to demoralize US troops. However, having a poor grasp of Hollywood undermined her effectiveness when she warned the invading forces: 'GI, why are you here? Don't you know you will die in the desert? While you are away, movie stars are taking your women. Robert Redford is dating your girlfriend. Tom Selleck is kissing your lady. Bart Simpson is making love to your wife.'

The British Navy once issued specific orders for the safe storage of warheads and torpedoes: 'It is necessary for technical reasons that these warheads should be stored with the top at the bottom and the bottom at the top. In order that there may be no doubt as to which is the top and which is the bottom, for storage purposes it will be seen that the bottom of each head has been labelled with the word "top".'

On 22 February 1940, a Luftwaffe bomber pilot was flying off the coast of the German island of Borkum when he noticed an enemy destroyer. Turning around he went into an attack position and dropped his bomb load on the ship. The vessel broke in half and sank with the loss of 280 of her crew.

The only problem was that the target turned out to be the *Leberecht Maass*, pride of the German navy. Sailing to its rescue, its sister ship, the *Max Schultz*, hit a mine and sank with the loss of her entire crew.

In 1986, in order to help its fight against the Soviet invasion, the CIA gave in the region of 1,000 shoulder-launched Stinger missiles to the Afghan rebels for free (they had actually cost $35,000 (£21,900) each). After the Russians withdrew from Afghanistan in 1989 the Afghan rebels started to sell the missiles for $100,000 (£62,500) each to Iran and North Korea. To prevent these weapons falling into enemy hands the CIA had to spend $65 million (£40 million) in order to buy them back.

During the Second World War the Pentagon developed a miniature incendiary bomb that could be strapped to a bat's body and then dropped over Japan. The idea was that the bats would land in the country's wooden homes and buildings and would then chew through string that held the bombs to their bodies, causing the bombs to fall and explode. A US Army test in New Mexico resulted in the bats landing in the wrong places and setting fire to the barracks and control tower of a brand-new and as yet unoccupied air force base, as well as setting alight a general's staff car. The project was abandoned.

FAIL

From 1981 to 1992 Sweden spent more than $480 million (£300 million) looking for Russian submarines exercising in its waters. Ships, surveillance aircraft, helicopters with sonar probes and teams of commandos and divers were all used to investigate the suspicious activity but no concrete evidence was ever found. According to a 1995 report by the Swedish Defence Ministry the intruders were most likely minks, pointing out that these animals have been known to produce the same sound patterns as submarines.

In March 1942 the British warship HMS *Trinidad* was on patrol in the Arctic Ocean when it spotted and then launched a torpedo at a German destroyer. The icy waters caused a gyroscope malfunction that sent the torpedo in a graceful arc back towards the *Trinidad* where it exploded, killing 32 of its crew and severely damaging the ship, which was eventually scuttled.

FAIL

During the 1982 Falklands War the Royal Air Force used US satellite imagery to show that it had effectively bombed Port Stanley's only runway, putting it out of action for the Argentinians. What they didn't realize was that in reality most of the 'destruction' was fake, created by Argentinian soldiers using heaps of earth to deceive the satellites. The replica craters were removed at night when the runway was operational, and then replaced at dawn.

German U-boat commander Wolfgang Lüth was the second most successful U-boat captain of the Second World War but met an inglorious end in 1945. Constantly aware of security issues he always gave strict instructions to guards to shoot anyone on sight who did not give the right password, regardless of any circumstances. He was shot by a sentry when he returned to Flensburg-Mürwik Naval Academy one day and gave the wrong password.

FAIL

In 1995 the US Defense Intelligence Agency admitted spending $20 million (£12.5 million) over the previous 17 years on psychics to help them locate Scud missile launchers being moved around by Saddam Hussein during Operation Desert Storm and also to find Americans being held hostage. The agency admitted that this programme hadn't achieved any significant results.

Launched with due pomp and ceremony in 1863, the USS *Keokuk* was billed as the world's first unsinkable battleship – a vital weapon for the north in the American civil war. Shaped like a modern submarine, the ship was designed so that any incoming shells would literally bounce off her armoured sides. The reality was not so effective; in her first action she managed to fire three rounds while receiving 90 direct hits from Confederate guns, including many below her waterline.

The *Keokuk* sank the next day.

[FAIL]

In October 1993, US Air Force pilot Lieutenant Colonel Don Snelgrove was flying his F-16 fighter jet over Turkey when he was caught short. Switching the jet to automatic pilot, he undid his lap belt so he could urinate into his 'piddle pack' – a pilot's emergency toilet, in reality just a plastic pouch containing a sponge.

Unfortunately the belt buckle became wedged between the control stick and his seat. As Snelgrove tried to free the buckle, the control stick shifted and the jet plunged from 33,000 feet to about 2,000 feet. Too low to regain control, all Snelgrove could do was eject just before his $18 million (£11.2 million) aircraft crashed – one of the most expensive visits to the toilet ever.

In 1968, at the height of the Vietnam War, the US Army began experimenting with ways to enhance soldiers' night vision. One of the proposals put forward didn't involve infra-red technology, but just plain old pussycats.

The plan was for cats to wear a special harness so they could lead foot patrols through the jungles in pitch-black conditions, just like guide dogs lead the blind. Military top brass approved the project and a trial began in Vietnam.

After about a month the army reported back to the Pentagon about the experiment. It turned out that these 'seeing-eye cats' had behaved in a thoroughly undisciplined manner, and it was just luck that no soldier had been killed or injured.

One squad, using four cats, was led in four completely different directions. Others found their cats running off in pursuit of mice and birds. If it was raining, the cats didn't want to go anywhere, but if they did, they'd usually give up leading the soldiers and instead play with the dangling straps of their backpacks as if it were some sort of toy.

It also turned out that several of the soldiers had traded their cats to Vietnamese women for 'favours', claiming that the animals had just 'run away'.

The scheme was soon abandoned.

After the First World War the French government embarked on an ambitious plan to establish a 400-mile-long series of defensive forts along its north-eastern border from Switzerland to Luxembourg to protect the country from another German invasion. It took ten years and an estimated three billion francs but by the time the Maginot Line was completed in 1939 the forts could house half a million soldiers and were linked by an underground railway. In 1940 the German army devised an ingenious plan to beat it. They cut through the Ardennes Forest in Belgium and overpowered the Maginot Line from behind.

LOST IN
TRANSLATION

> '*We are all failures. At least the best of us are.*'
>
> J. M. BARRIE

Not so much 'two cultures separated by a common language', as 'two cultures separated by idiots in the marketing department – or those who don't understand the locals...'

[FAIL]

When Kentucky Fried Chicken opened its first outlet in Beijing in 1987, its slogan 'Finger lickin' good' was incorrectly translated into Chinese characters that meant literally, 'Eat your fingers off'.

☹

When Gerber started selling baby food in Africa the company used the same packaging as in the United States with an illustration of the cute Gerber baby on the label. Slow sales prompted an investigation. What Gerber didn't realize was that in Africa where many customers are illiterate, companies label jars and packages with photos that represent the contents.

A widely reported story in the 1990s concerns a department store in the shopping district of Ginza, Tokyo, organizing a topical window display in December to appeal to western visitors – and confusing the two most prominent images associated with Christmas: Jesus Christ and Santa Claus.

The result was a very disturbing life-size mannequin of Santa on a crucifix.

President Jimmy Carter gave a short speech when he arrived at Warsaw Airport in December 1977. However, his translator managed to completely mangle Carter's statement: 'I have come to learn your opinions and understand your desires for the future.' What came out was: 'I desire the Pole carnally.'

In 1988, the General Electric Company (GEC) and the British company Plessey combined forces to create a new telecommunications giant. The new corporation was named GPT for GEC-Plessey Telecommunications. However, it was hard for the firm to be taken seriously in France where GPT is pronounced in French as *J'ai pété*, or 'I've farted'.

Early advertisements for Coca-Cola's bottled water Dasani called it 'bottled spunk' or featured the tag line 'Can't live without spunk'. Coca-Cola seemed oblivious to the slang meaning for spunk in the UK. Fortunately, the ads were soon dropped.

In 1996 Matsushita Electric, parent company of Panasonic, was promoting a Japanese PC that came with a Japanese web browser featuring the cartoon character Woody Woodpecker as the user-friendly internet guide.

The day before the start of a national marketing campaign (which would eventually be rolled out worldwide), Panasonic cancelled the product launch after it was pointed out how the launch slogan might be deemed inappropriate in the United States. The proposed phrase was: 'Touch Woody – The Internet Pecker'.

(FAIL)

In the 1980s Coors Light used the slogan 'Turn it loose'. The advertising agency mistranslated this for the American Hispanic market and the phrase instead came out as, 'Suffer from diarrhoea'.

In the late 1970s, the American computer company Wang was puzzled and somewhat annoyed when its British subsidiary refused to use the company's latest slogan, 'Wang Cares'.

(FAIL)

It's reported that in April 2003 the Hong Kong Tourist Board tried to pull its ads and change its latest billboard campaign because of the featured slogan: 'Hong Kong: It will take your breath away'. The campaign unfortunately coincided with the deadly SARS epidemic sweeping the region, a major symptom of which was shortness of breath.

When Pillsbury marketed its Jolly Green Giant sweetcorn products in Saudi Arabia, 'Jolly Green Giant' got translated literally into Arabic as 'Intimidating Green Ogre'.

One of the most useless yet comical phrase books was *The New Guide of the Conversation in Portuguese and English*, created by Pedro Carolino in 1883. Mr Carolino had little or no command of English but what he did have was a Portuguese–French dictionary and a French–English dictionary. What he thought would be a simple task of cross-referencing words among the three languages resulted in some of the most bizarre phrases ever devised, including:
    'Exculpate me by your brother's.'
    'He laughs at my nose, he jest by me.'
    'Comb me quick.'
    'To craunch a marmoset.'
    'Nothing some money, nothing of Swiss.'

When the US National Dairy Council rolled out its famous 'Got Milk?' campaign for the Hispanic market the slogan was translated as '*¿Tiene leche?*' This actually means 'Are you lactating?'

When the US National Dairy Council rolled out its famous 'Got Milk?' campaign for the Hispanic market the slogan was translated as '*¿Tiene leche?*' This actually means 'Are you lactating?'

In 1977 when Braniff Airlines ran radio commercials in Spanish promoting its luxury seating with the slogan 'Fly in leather', it failed to realize that when spoken, the slogan sounded identical to the Spanish for 'Fly naked'.

[FAIL]

Founder and CEO of the chicken business that shares his name, Frank Perdue's American slogan, 'It takes a tough man to make a tender chicken,' ended up embarrassing him when it was mistranslated into Spanish. A photograph of Perdue with one of his birds appeared on billboards all over Mexico with a caption that explained, 'It takes a hard man to make a chicken aroused.'

In 1770 Captain James Cook landed in Australia and asked the Aborigines what they called the unusual-looking jumping marsupials he'd seen. He was told 'kangaroo' and the name stuck. Cook never realized that this is just Aborigine for 'I don't understand you.'

When Coca-Cola was first sold in China in 1927, the drink's name had to be translated into Chinese characters. To find the nearest phonetic equivalent to 'Coca-Cola' required a separate Chinese character for each of the four syllables. Characters that made the sound, 'ko-ka-ko-la' soon appeared on Chinese shop signs around the country. It wasn't until much later that the company discovered the symbols meant 'bite the wax tadpole' or 'female horse stuffed with wax' depending on the dialect.

Pepsi was not immune to local mistranslations, either. In Taiwan, the translation of the Pepsi slogan 'Come alive with the Pepsi Generation' came out as 'Pepsi will bring your ancestors back from the dead'.

FAIL

Although disputed by the company, it's often reported that when General Motors launched its Chevy Nova across Latin America in the 1960s, company executives were surprised by its relatively low sales. Then it was pointed out that, in Spanish, 'no va' means 'doesn't go'.

Similar examples of car names being lost in translation include the Mitsubishi Pajero (a word that means masturbator in Spanish), the Honda Fitta (introduced to Nordic countries in 2001 where the word is slang for female genitalia – it was renamed the Honda Jazz) and the Ford Pinto (in Brazilian Portuguese slang, *pinto* means small penis).

Launching its products in Mexico, Parker Pen's ad agency mistranslated the phrase 'Won't leak in your pocket and embarrass you', so it read instead: 'Won't leak in your pocket and make you pregnant.'

PLANES, TRAINS AND AUTOMOBILES (AND SHIPS)

> *'I never fail. It's just that the people around me succeed more than I.'*
>
> CARROLL BRYANT

Travel might broaden the mind but it doesn't eliminate the chance of experiencing some form of mishap or failure. Suddenly your own two feet seem like the best mode of transport going...

On Christmas Day 1994 Nigerian bus driver Niyi Owoeye was driving near the town of Akure when he saw an antelope wandering at the side of the road. Thinking this would make a good trophy, Owoeye swerved his bus and ran it over. It was only when he got out to inspect the damage he'd caused that Owoeye realized the antelope was in fact Mr Ratimi Alesanmi, a member of the Nigerian Federal Commission for Road Safety.

Pilot Christian Kaget was preparing to land at a Mozambique airport, but when he radioed the control tower to announce his descent, all he could hear was a loud tapping sound. Thinking this was interference and concerned he wouldn't be able to reach the tower, Kaget then contacted the airport authorities. The airport manager and other officials rushed to the control tower where they discovered the sole air traffic controller, Luther Ungumbe, dancing on one of the desks wearing red patent tap shoes. He was arrested and later dismissed.

In 2005 the £200-million luxury liner *Aurora* was the flagship of the P&O fleet and was due to set sail from Southampton in what had been billed as a 'Grand Voyage' – a 103-night cruise visiting 40 ports in 23 countries.

In the end the cruise lasted just 11 days and only visited one port: Southampton.

From the moment she was due to set sail on 9 January, the pride of the P&O fleet was plagued by a catalogue of engine problems and failures, first reaching as far as the Isle of Wight before having to return to Southampton. A slew of disasters followed and on 19 January, ten days after she was meant to depart, the *Aurora* had only reached as far as 25 miles off the Devon coast – at which point P&O decided to cut its losses and cancel the cruise for which passengers had paid between £9,800 and £41,985 for the 'trip of a lifetime'.

A British Airways promotion in 1981 offered honeymoon trips to St Lucia. It stated that the hotel prices were based on 'four or five people sharing'.

The 164-mile Jingshi expressway linking Beijing and Shijiazhuang used to have a middle lane that cars on both sides of the road were allowed to use. This made head-on collisions inevitable if two drivers travelling in opposite directions decided to try and pass at the same time. During the first year of the expressway 404 people died and 1,028 were injured.

FAIL

Police in the town of Natchitoches, Louisiana, arrested Simpson Williams Jr after he deliberately drove his Mercedes into their Chevrolet patrol car. When questioned on the motive for his behaviour Williams told authorities that his German car had told him to kill an American-made vehicle.

Glen Woodcock was proud of his Ford Bronco and was extremely upset, not to say anxious, when he accidentally drove it on to a US Army firing range near Fort Bragg, North Carolina, and got stuck. He was arrested by military police after being seen walking on the range which was littered with unexploded ammunition. The garrison commander Colonel Wilson commented, 'Why or how he did not step on something and blow himself totally up is a miracle.' Unfortunately for Mr Woodrow it was deemed too dangerous to retrieve his car and it was left on the range as a target.

[FAIL]

In June 1999 an unnamed woman took delivery of a new 22-foot Bayliner motor yacht. However, on taking it out in Lake Isabella, California, she found it sluggish and hard to manoeuvre – nothing like she had expected. Frustrated and annoyed at its performance she sailed it to the marina so it could be checked. The engine and propeller were in perfect working order so one of the mechanics jumped in to inspect the boat below the waterline.

There he discovered the problem. When the owner put her boat into the lake it was still securely attached to the trailer.

A Russian man by the name of E. Frenkel believed he had extraordinary mental powers, claiming that he had been able to stop a bike, a car and then a streetcar with the power of his mind – and that his next feat would be to stop an express train. Walking alongside a railway track in the town of Astrakan near the Volga River he stepped into the path of an approaching train with his arms raised.

The official report read: 'Emergency braking failed to help. A tragedy occurred.'

In 1987, while making a film about the importance of wearing seat belts, Anthony Galati suffered serious head injuries after being involved in a car crash in Los Angeles. He was not wearing a seat belt.

Pierre Morache of Carcassone in France acted as the Good Samaritan when he helped three youths push-start a car. He failed to realize it was actually his own car until it started and disappeared down the street right in front of his very eyes.

Houston school bus driver Lillie Baltrip was pleased to receive a safe driving award in 1988. En route to the acceptance ceremony and driving a bus containing 29 other school bus drivers, she took a corner too sharply and overturned her vehicle. Baltrip and 16 of her passengers were taken to hospital after the accident.

In 1995 an Aeroflot charter plane crashed near Baku, the capital of Azerbaijan, after its crew forgot to refuel it at its previous stop.

[FAIL]

When a light aircraft crash-landed on the runway at Toledo Express Airport in Ohio, it went unnoticed by airport staff and even those in the control tower for more than 30 minutes. In the end one of the plane's occupants got out of the wreckage and walked over to the airport's main terminal, where he reported the accident.

In 1981 a Lanarkshire man named Mr Thomson arrived at his local driving test centre and sounded his horn to attract the attention of the examiner and tell him he was ready to start his test. The examiner approached Mr Thomson, told him that it was illegal to sound the horn while the car was stationary, then failed him.

[FAIL]

Loading and unloading crates and containers on the quayside is a difficult job, but Pierre Joilot, who worked at the busy Toulouse Docks seemed to find it more difficult than most, managing to drive his forklift truck over the edge of the wharf. Once can be put down to bad luck or extenuating circumstances, but after it happened two or three times, his employers' patience began to grow thin. It was only after the sixth time it happened that they sacked him.

The British hypnotist Romark was so convinced of his psychic powers that he announced in 1977 that he would drive a car through Ilford blindfolded. In October of that year his eyes were completely covered and he set off in his Renault down Cranbrook Road. Approximately 20 yards later he hit a parked police van, which ended his demonstration.

He later commented, 'The van was parked in a place that logic told me it wouldn't be.'

A similar incident occurred in Ottawa when 27-year-old Lauren Rhodes, claiming to have X-ray vision, attempted to prove it by driving blindfolded down a city street. She managed to run over the foot of a pedestrian, knock down a streetlight and crash into three vehicles, one of which was a police car. She was fined the equivalent of £400 and banned from driving for two years.

Abner Kriller of Albany, Australia, was out in his car one day in 1995 when he discovered he shouldn't really be driving and chewing gum at the same time. The huge bubble he'd just blown burst in his face, covering him with pink goo and temporarily blinding him. He failed to see an approaching bend and crashed off a clifftop.

In 1999 67-year-old farmer's wife Betty Stobbs from Durham was killed when a flock of sheep stampeded towards her quad bike, pushing her over the edge of Ashes Quarry in Stanhope. She survived the 100-foot fall, only to be crushed by the falling bike.

In 1994 Frank and Marie Moor of Bournemouth in Dorset set off for a caravanning holiday in France but managed to forget one thing: their caravan. Their error was spotted by their son, who noticed the caravan still in their garden after seeing them off. The couple only realized their mistake when a local radio station broadcast a message telling them to look in their rear-view mirror.

Sir Peter Parker, then chairman of British Rail, was on his way to an important meeting with Cumbria County Council in July 1978 but managed to board the wrong train at Crewe. Realizing his mistake he wrote a note around a coin and threw it on to the platform as the train passed through Tamworth station in Staffordshire (these were pre-mobile phone days). The note said, 'Please apologize to Cumbria Council and tell them I won't be able to make it.' Sir Peter reached London and the next time he set off for the meeting he went by plane.

IN CASE OF EMERGENCY

> '*I didn't fail the test, I just found one hundred ways to do it wrong.*'
>
> BENJAMIN FRANKLIN

Cool under pressure, knowledgeable and competent? You'd expect this of the police, fire and ambulance services. In some cases, though, you'd be very wrong...

FAIL

When road contractors accidentally laid tarmac over a series of water hydrants in Bath pavements, a senior fireman was given the task of locating them with a special metal detector. The first one was found quickly but when the tarmac was dug up, there was nothing beneath it. The same thing happened again . . . and again . . . and again. It was only after seven holes had been dug that the fireman realized that the metal detector was being set off by his boots' steel toecaps.

After Atlanta fire inspectors had completed a thorough survey of the Winecoff Hotel in 1946, they proudly designated it 'absolutely fireproof'. Shortly afterward it burned to the ground.

[FAIL]

It seemed like a good idea at the time, teaching police officers in Waukegan, Illinois, the correct way to reduce injuries while subduing offenders. However, in the six-hour class three officers were injured at the hands of colleagues while a fourth broke his toe tripping over one of the foam training mats.

In December 1995 fire officers from Rotherham's Red Watch were practising how to rescue people stuck in a lift. As part of the drill, 11 of them piled into a lift in Beversleigh flats in the town, only for it to get stuck between floors. They sounded the alarm and were eventually rescued by officers from the neighbouring Darnell fire station. Red Watch had become red-faced.

[FAIL]

Firemen called to an emergency at the home of Richard Derrick in Taunton in 1990 were extinguishing a fire when the glass in Richard's 80-gallon aquarium cracked from the heat, depositing 60 valuable tropical fish on the carpet. A quick-thinking fireman quickly scooped them up and immediately put them in another large fish tank in the room. He didn't realize this tank was home to Percy the Piranha, who proceeded to have his lunch.

On the night of 27 November 2008 the burglar alarm sounded at the PNC Bank in Montgomery Township, New Jersey. Although the blinds were drawn police caught sight of what was described as a 'menacing and a shadowy figure' inside. Concerned that an armed robbery was in progress they called in a heavily armed SWAT team, who sealed the area and evacuated local residents. With a spotter helicopter hovering overhead they stormed the premises and apprehended the shadowy figure: a cardboard cut-out of a man in a suit used to promote the bank's low-cost finance deals.

In March 1986 police in Indianapolis arrested a women for passing $100,000-worth (£62,500) of bad cheques, then allowed her to post bail – with a cheque. No sooner had she done this than she was on the run before the police discovered the inevitable: this cheque also bounced.

A police road-safety bus was unable to make an appearance at a fair in Earlsheaton, West Yorkshire, in June 1993 where it was scheduled to offer advice and displays about safer driving. The reason? It was involved in an accident en route – but not just any old accident. This one involved it colliding with a 17-ton lorry, a motorbike, a car and another bus.

To warn members of the public about the dangers of brush fires started by careless Independence Day celebrations, members of the San Diego police force and firefighters decided to destroy thousands of illegal fireworks in front of assembled reporters. Gathering at a remote bomb-disposal range outside the city the hoard of fireworks was blown up. However, stray sparks caused a ten-acre brush fire that required 50 firefighters and two water-dropping helicopters to put it out.

Mark Small, a paramedic from Bristol, boasted on Facebook that during a night shift for the Great Western Ambulance Service he groped a patient's breasts while resuscitating her. His post said, 'Saved someone's life and managed to cop a feel of some cracking jubblies.'

His comments were seen and reported and Small appeared before the Health Professions Council, which found his fitness to practice impaired and placed him under caution. Shannett Thompson, a spokesperson for the Council commented, 'The term "jubblies", I'm led to believe, relates to a woman's breast area.'

Stockholm's police college had to cancel a training session on dealing with drunk drivers because half of the trainee officers due to attend had been out drinking the night before and officials doubted that they were sober enough to drive to class. The academy head instructor Krister Nyberg commented, 'We must have limits. You can't be at the police academy while smelling of alcohol.'

Jeffrey Hoffman, a 23-year-old police cadet, stabbed fellow cadet Nick Berrena to death in January 1998 after trying to prove that his knife wouldn't penetrate Berrena's flak vest. It did.

In a similar incident a security guard at a Moscow bank asked a colleague to try and stab him in order to test his protective vest. It turned out it wasn't as protective as he thought and he died of a heart wound.

[FAIL]

As part of an entrapment policy operated by the Northumbrian police force, a specially adapted Ford Sierra was left invitingly unlocked around the streets of Newcastle upon Tyne. The engine was designed to cut out after just 20 yards, at which point the doors and windows would also lock, trapping thieves until the police arrived.

In October 1992 it was driven away from where it had been parked in the city – and was never located. All the police would say was that there had been a 'malfunction'.

A Washington DC housing agency was a bit overzealous when it came to publicizing a successful drugs raid by FBI officers and the police on one of its public housing complexes: it issued a press release the night before the supposedly top-secret operation.

The raid, which involved over 200 officers, had to be called off as the FBI agent in charge heard the covert mission announced on the radio as he was driving to the staging area; six months of careful planning and hundreds of thousands of dollars were wasted.

Admitting its blunder, the housing agency later stated that the error 'in no way diminishes our commitment to assist law enforcement agencies.'

A massive explosion in the headquarters of the Philippines' National Bureau of Investigation in Manila in August 1999 was first attributed to a terrorist attack. The blast killed seven people and demolished the offices of the NBI Special Investigation Division. But the ensuing inquiry came to the conclusion that the explosion was in fact caused by one of the NBI's own agents. It turned out that he had extinguished a cigarette in a fire bucket, as was his usual practice. This time, however, he didn't realize that someone had decided to store seized explosives there.

FAIL

As a ploy to deter crime in Stockport, Greater Manchester, the local police force decided to put a life-size cardboard cut-out of one of its officers, Bob Malloy, outside a Sainsbury's – the thought being that even a fake policeman would make would-be shoplifters and other criminals think again.

It was stolen.

In October 1994 prison officers at a Florida jail had so much faith in their highly trained and intelligent new tracker dog that they offered double murderer David Graham a chance to test it. They let him out with a 30-minute head start before they released their dog. The dog failed to find him and local police were then called in to assist. Graham was never seen again.

After a police helicopter picked up a tell-tale heat signature in January 2011, six officers descended on a cannabis farm in Bradford – a garage belonging to Pam Hardcastle. Ordering her to open the door they saw the garage wasn't filled with illegal drugs being cultivated. Instead it was occupied by Simon and Kenny, two pet guinea pigs belonging to her ten-year-old son, Jack, and a heater to keep them warm.

Coastguards on the Firth of Forth ignored a sequence of flares they saw off the small island of Inchkeith on Halloween 1992. Only after reports came in about a badly damaged boat did they launch a lifeboat. The flares had been fired by William and George Redpath, whose 21-foot yacht had been holed on the rocks after suffering engine trouble. When asked why the coastguards had initially ignored the distress signal they admitted that they thought the flares were part of some weird ritual, commenting, 'The island is supposed to be connected with witchcraft.'

[FAIL]

Lieutenant Colonel Julio Ramon Rivera was incensed after police in El Salvador arrested three Salvadorian employees of the US Embassy for drinking and carrying weapons. Arriving at the station he wanted to prove that the weapons were all replicas and proceeded to pull the pin on a grenade. It was, of course, real and the resultant explosion killed Rivera, two police officers and two of the detained employees.

In September 1994 an undercover police operation was in progress outside Cundall village hall in Yorkshire, where a meeting of the Animal Rights Militia was in progress. The venue had been under surveillance for a while, and when two of the ARM members went outside for a cigarette break, the police pounced, questioning them about the latest violent exploits being planned.

It was then that detectives discovered that they'd got the wrong ARM. The hall was hosting a meeting of the Association of Radical Midwives, who were discussing, among other things, progressive home-birth plans.

MEDICAL MISHAPS

They say that the doctor is to be feared more than the disease – from the evidence of these medical blunders we'd have to agree with that...

[FAIL]

In November 1974, 42-year-old Virginia O'Hare of New York went to see plastic surgeon Howard Bellin for a simple tummy-tuck operation. Afterwards she discovered that her belly button had been moved two inches off-centre. She successfully sued for malpractice.

☹

English author Arnold Bennett was visiting Paris in 1931 when he downed a glass of water in front of friends in order to prove it was safe to drink. He contracted typhoid from it and subsequently died.

A railway accident in Munich resulted in 11 passengers receiving serious injuries, including two who lost their hands. Doctors who arrived on the scene quickly managed to retrieve the hands, pack them on ice and later reattach them – unfortunately not to their original owners. The mix-up was only discovered after surgery was complete – and occurred due to both victims having the same blood type. According to a hospital spokesman, 'One of the patients wants his original hands back, but we're trying to talk him out of that.' Whether they were successful or not is unrecorded.

A Dublin woman visited her GP complaining of a bad cough and was prescribed a combination of antibiotics and cough medicine. He also gave her a free sample of the medicine, supplied by the manufacturers. She returned four days later complaining that she found the cough medicine 'vile and sickening', and was feeling worse than when she originally came in.

The GP looked at the bottle he'd given her and realized it was a urine sample given to him by another patient. The woman sued the practice for £22,000.

FAIL

At least a hundred men in Thailand were revealed to have undergone bogus penis-enlargement operations, according to the *Bangkok Post*. The paper reported that the so-called doctors who performed the surgery injected the men's penises with a mixture of olive oil, chalk and other unknown substances to provide bulk. One official at a hospital in Chiang Mai told the paper, 'I've even seen penises containing bits of the Bangkok telephone directory.'

Russian physician Alexander Bogdanov started a series of blood transfusion experiments in 1924, supposedly hoping to achieve eternal youth. Spurred on by his apparent success (including the improvement of his eyesight and a halt to his baldness), he exchanged blood with a young student to see if he could absorb any of his youthfulness. Unfortunately the student was suffering from TB and malaria. Bogdanov died, but the student injected with his blood made a complete recovery.

$$\boxed{\text{FAIL}}$$

Brazilian farm worker Francisco Asis dos Santos had an unorthodox approach to try and stop his toothache: he tried to shoot the tooth out with his gun. According to the Globo News Network he managed instead to shoot out his eye – but sadly the tooth remained.

Being a witch doctor, the uncle of Servando Rodriguez of Houston knew exactly what to do after his nephew complained about constant back pain. His cure involved placing cotton balls soaked in rubbing alcohol in a jar, igniting these and placing the upturned jar on his nephew's back. As the flames were extinguished due to lack of oxygen they would draw all the pain out.

It all seemed straightforward, if a little unconventional, but according to Sgt. John Denholm of Harris County Sheriff's Department, it all went wrong after the uncle left the cure in the hands of his landlord's wife. Misunderstanding the procedure she was rubbing the alcohol into Servando's back when her cigarette accidentally ignited it. Leaping up, she spilled the rest of the alcohol, which also caught fire. Servando later died from burns to his back and groin.

Milorad Jovanic entered a Vienna hospital for treatment for his rheumatism but during his stay he tripped and broke a leg. After it was set he was taken by mistake into the pre-op ward. Soon after that he was wheeled into an operating theatre and anaesthetized before he could protest at what was happening. When he awoke Jovanic discovered he'd been confused with another patient and ended up having a heart pacemaker fitted. He then had to wait another three weeks until he was fit enough to have another operation to remove the pacemaker.

In 1995, just before he was due to have his gangrenous right foot amputated, 52-year-old Willie King joked with staff at the University Community Hospital in Tampa, Florida to make sure they operated on the correct one. He awoke from the operation to find his infected foot still present ... and his healthy left foot missing. The result was that he ended up with both legs amputated just below the knee, settling with the hospital for $900,000 (£562,000). After the incident, the hospital introduced a sophisticated system to make sure this tragic event never reoccurred; they would write a large 'NO' on limbs that were not to be removed.

[FAIL]

An anonymous male individual got a vibrator stuck in his rectum, but rather than risk the embarrassment of the local emergency room decided to try and fish the object out himself using a pair of salad tongs. It was only when these, too, became stuck that he turned himself over to medical professionals.

A Second World War veteran suffered such bad haemorrhoids that in order to alleviate the problem, he would push them back in with an old artillery shell from an anti-aircraft gun. On one occasion, though, he used too much force and the shell got stuck, forcing him to make an embarrassing visit to his local emergency room. Just before the removal operation, one of the doctors casually asked, 'It is spent, isn't it?' 'Oh, no!' admitted the soldier. 'There's enough ammo in that shell to blast a Messerschmitt out of the sky.' The surgical team was forced to notify an army bomb squad and a lead box had to be built around the patient's bottom, then the live shell defused before it could be successfully removed.

[FAIL]

The British Migraine Association once distributed 13,000 car stickers to its members. However, a constituent of the ink that had been used caused instant migraine attacks in many sufferers. One recipient collapsed just from opening the envelope.

In 2009 Romanian surgeon, Naum Ciomu, was operating on patient Nelu Radonescu, 36, to correct a testicular malformation when he suddenly lost his temper. Grabbing a scalpel, he sliced off his patient's penis in front of shocked nursing staff and threw it on to the operating table, where he proceeded to chop it into small pieces before storming out of the Bucharest hospital. The surgeon blamed his actions on stress and told a medical tribunal that it was a temporary loss of judgement due to personal problems.

Mr Redonescu received £100,000 compensation plus damages to finance an operation to rebuild his penis using tissue from his arm.

Dr Mark MacDonald was working late one night in the ER when a man ran in and yelled, 'My wife's going to have her baby in the cab!' The doctor grabbed his bag, rushed out to the cab and lifted the lady's dress. That's when he noticed there were several cabs parked outside – and he was in the wrong one.

An elderly woman in Tennessee complained of a sharp pain in her buttocks and after X-rays were taken, it was diagnosed as a tumour that required immediate removal. During the operation surgeons discovered that the tumour they were expecting was actually a pork chop bone.

The patient didn't remember ever being naked and sitting on it but doctors estimated it had been there for at least five years.

A Georgia attorney who had been admitted to his local emergency room told staff he'd been making a call with his cell phone in the shower when he slipped and accidentally fell on the phone, resulting in it becoming lodged in an unfortunate place. What should have been a relatively straightforward operation to remove the device ended up taking far longer than it should have. According to reports the phone rang three times during the operation and each time, the surgical team collapsed into hysterics and had to wait until they'd regained their composure before carrying on the procedure.

After complaining of severe dizziness and difficulty walking a London woman was told by her doctor that she was exhibiting the symptoms of tertiary syphilis. As you might imagine, the patient was exceptionally worried by this diagnosis. However, on further examination it turned out that she was just suffering from 'wobbly shoes' and once she changed to a new pair, her 'symptoms' disappeared.

Ironically named Jason Luck, a 22-year-old Worthing lifeguard, fell out of a moving train and over a viaduct in 1992 but miraculously survived. However, his troubles began – and ended – in hospital. It was here that he accidentally fell out of a high window, where his severe injuries led to him being connected to a life-support machine – which failed to ring an alarm when a tube came loose, finally killing him.

Joan Morris, a 67-year-old woman, was admitted to a teaching hospital after she fell and banged her head. A scan showed she had two aneurysms, which were successfully removed by surgery. Mrs Morris was transferred to a different ward to await discharge the following day. The next morning, however, she was collected by porters and whisked into an operating theatre where she underwent open-heart surgery. Just over an hour later, a doctor from a different department called and asked what the heart surgeon was doing with his patient. Once the mistake was realized, the operation was stopped and Mrs Morris was returned to her room in what the hospital claimed was a stable condition.

LOSING MY RELIGION

Some people put a little too much faith in the Almighty and are surprised when things don't go according to plan. It just goes to prove that God does move in mysterious ways...

Soul singer/songwriter Donnie Hathaway would often sing and preach the gospel by leaning out of his 17-floor Chicago apartment and also from hotel windows wherever he stayed. This happened until 13 January 1979, when he leaned too far out of the 15th-floor window of the Essex House Hotel in New York, and died of multiple fractures from his fall.

[FAIL]

In 2002 a Jehovah's Witness decided to tell passing motorists about God's glory by running out into the middle of Interstate 55 in Illinois. This was not her first attempt to spread the Word, but after she was hit by a speeding car, it was definitely her last.

FAIL

The cult People Unlimited believed its members could achieve immortality purely by the power of thought. After the death of three of its fellow worshippers, spokesperson Beryl Gregory defended the group's credibility, claiming that the three dead members didn't believe hard enough.

In May 1994 the Pakistani Islamic sect of Tebrik-e-Nifaz announced that its members should drive on the right-hand side of the road. The followers did as their leaders decreed. The problem was that all other Pakistanis drive on the left.

After a fortnight of accidents and near-misses the sect renounced its orders.

FAIL

Maria Benoiza Nascimento, an unemployed cleaner and mother of seven, was told by her priest that if she continued to gamble by playing the lottery she would go to hell. With his words still ringing in her ears she burned the lottery ticket she had just bought. Had she kept the ticket she would have won the equivalent of $60,000 (£37,500).

Religious extremist Leonso Canales of Kingsville, Texas, tried in vain to get the word 'hello' banned from everyday use, claiming, 'I see "hell" in "hello". It's disguised by the "o", but once you see it, it will slap you in the face.' He wanted the greeting changed to 'heaveno'. His prayers weren't answered.

The 'Wicked Bible' published in London in 1631 was so-called because of a printing error. In Exodus 20:14 the seventh commandment reads: 'Thou shalt commit adultery.'

Elders at the North Waterboro Community Baptist Church in Maine couldn't work out why some younger congregants were sniggering as they went to church. It might have been the large illuminated welcome sign that read, 'You can't enter heaven unless Jesus enters you.'

Italian priest Don Giacomo Perlnl was standing outside his church in Alto Adige cursing the storms that had been plaguing the town when the foundations of a huge cross in the churchyard, loosened by the torrential rainfall, caused it to crash down on him.

FAIL

A beautiful stained-glass window at All Saints Church, Oystermouth, Mumbles, Swansea, had remained hidden from view for over 90 years until it was unexpectedly revealed by renovation work in 1994. The day before its highly awaited official unveiling a workman accidentally smashed it with a scaffolding pole. The vicar, canon Geoff Thomas, was appropriately forgiving and philosophical, commenting, 'Stained glass is broken so easily.'

In 1870 Pope Pius IX blessed a ship full of nuns heading to South America. It sank en route, drowning everyone on board.

FAIL

In 1988 American preacher Paul Wren decided on a novel way to demonstrate the strength of the Lord working through him – by picking up a member of his congregation with his teeth. The person he chose, however, was 27-stone Joe Pearce. Before he bent over to pick up Mr Pearce in a specially designed harness, Wren announced, 'I do this to make you realize how the Lord can give you great strength and how uplifting he can be.'

The attempt was not successful and all that happened was that Pearce remained grounded – and Wren lost five of his teeth. He mumbled through the rest of his sermon and then left the church quickly to find an emergency dentist, reflecting, 'I'll have to find a new way to prove the power of the Lord.'

Religious fanatic Alessandro Bartok of Verona was on holiday with his family in Germany driving on the autobahn, boring his family rigid about the glory of Jesus. His son did not share his strong belief, so in an attempt to demonstrate the powers of the Messiah, Mr Bartok removed his hands from the steering wheel, asking Jesus to 'Drive your servants home.'

Whatever powers the Holy Spirit possessed that day, driving wasn't one of them. The car suddenly zigzagged across all lanes of the motorway before crashing into the back of a lorry, causing an 18-car pile up. Mr Bartok's faith was not shaken and he declared the fact that no one had been killed was 'a miracle'.

A 91-year-old woman named Adelaide Douglas of Queensland, Australia, got quite a shock when she opened a package containing what she thought was a statuette of the Virgin Mary from AVA Enterprises. The box actually contained a nine-inch dildo and a sex manual. A spokesman for the company explained that they deal in both religious trinkets and sex aids and that unfortunately, mix-ups sometimes occurred...

[FAIL]

California-based Christian radio broadcaster Harold Camping gained notoriety after predicting that the end of the world would take place on 21 May 2011. On 22 May he sheepishly emerged from his house saying he was 'flabbergasted' that this hadn't happened and that he was 'looking for answers'. He then revised his prediction and announced that the date would definitely be 21 October the same year. In March 2012 he stated that his attempt to predict a date was 'sinful'.

When DeWitt Finley got stuck in a heavy snowdrift in autumn 1994 while trying to travel through the Klamath Mountains in northern California, he put his faith in God. The devoutly religious man decided to stay in his pick-up truck, convinced someone would soon rescue him. He sat there for nine weeks, ticking off the days in his diary and writing letters to his nearest and dearest, until some time in mid-January 1995 he finally died of starvation. He wasn't actually found until May that year, which is when rescuers discovered he had never even left his vehicle. If he had, he would have discovered a clear road leading down from the mountain just a few yards away.

[FAIL]

The wife of doomsday cult leader Gerhard Wolff, 58, from Dresden in Germany, decided to play a practical joke on her husband by writing the number '666' on his forehead while he was asleep. On waking up Wolff looked in the bathroom mirror, saw the number of the beast – and hanged himself. The note he left his wife read, 'The devil has me in his grip. There is no escape.'

[FAIL]

The Brixton Action Station theatre company planned to stage a play called *CruciFiction* in 1986, a sensational retelling of the Easter story, but the production was plagued with problems from the start. The first Jesus was knocked off his bike by a lorry and broke his leg. His replacement slipped on an icy pavement and broke his arm. Judas had to leave after his father tried to commit suicide, then Peter, John and James left after a big argument with the director.

Fearing that the play was cursed, the rest of the actors left and the whole play had to be re-cast. Nine days before curtain-up, the latest Jesus and Mary Magdalene walked out during the read-through when they discovered that in this version of the Easter miracle, Jesus was an alcoholic. This was the final straw for the theatre company's director, who promptly had a nervous breakdown. The whole show was then cancelled.

BAD BEHAVIOUR

Mad, bad and dangerous to know ... how about dim-witted and stupid, too?

FAIL

Patrick Doyle attended a trial in Fonda, New York, wearing a T-shirt that read, 'If shit could fly this place would be an airport.' Even though he was appearing as a witness, the judge sentenced him to 30 days for contempt of court.

In a similar story, Jeremiah Johnson appeared in Polk County courthouse in Florida to answer a charge of driving without a licence but was refused entry by the court bailiff because he was wearing shorts. He left but returned a few moments later without his shorts or in fact, any other item of clothing. The presiding judge sentenced him to 179 days in jail.

It was a very drunk Gerard Finneran, the 58-year-old head of a US investment bank, who was travelling first class from Buenos Aires to New York in 1995. After being refused any more alcohol Finneran became abusive to the airline staff and climbed on top of the beverage trolley, where he proceeded to drop his trousers and defecate, using linen napkins as toilet paper, then, as the airline later stated in court, 'tracking faeces throughout the aircraft'. At his trial he was sentenced to 300 hours of community service and handed a $50,000 (£31,000) cleaning bill. Finneran promised the judge, 'you will never hear of me doing anything like this again.'

In 2001 Peter Chung, a city financier, moved from London to take up a lucrative new post with the Carlyle Group, a private equity group based in Seoul, South Korea. In May that year he sent an email to his friends bragging about his post and his sexual exploits, asking them to send him boxes of condoms, claiming that he'd brought out about 40 but that he thought he'd run out of them by Saturday. In the email he boasted that: 'I pretty much get about, on average, five to eight phone numbers a night and at least three hot chicks that say that they want to go home with me every night I go out.' He also explained why he needed a three-bedroom apartment: 'The main bedroom is for my queen-size bed, where Chung is going to f**k every hot chick in Korea over the next two years. The second bedroom is for my harem of chickies, and the third bedroom is for all of you f**kers when you come out to visit my ass in Korea.'

His friends re-circulated his email, and after it had been read by almost everyone on Wall Street, *The New York Times* wrote a story on it. When asked to comment on the effect of his bragging, Peter told the newspaper that it was devastating and he'd had no option but to resign from his dream job.

After James Dyer and Audrey Plummer met in a Frinton pub and hit it off they decided to go to the hottest club in town: the Cat's Whisker Nitespot. Unfortunately, James was refused entry as he was wearing jeans and didn't have a tie. Wanting to impress his date he told her to wait outside for a few minutes. He then walked to a nearby clothes shop, threw a brick through the window and turned up shortly afterwards at the club wearing an expensive three-piece suit, a silk shirt and tie. The police arrived at the club shortly afterwards and arrested James. The next day, while still in police custody, he proposed to Audrey. She told her local newspaper that she was 'thinking it over'.

FAIL

Italian Claudio Ferro decided that it would be easier for him to get a job if he had some sort of disability, so in 1975 he decided to fake blindness. The ruse worked and he soon landed a job as a switchboard operator after turning up at an interview with a white stick and wearing dark glasses. 'They were extremely kind,' Mr Ferro said about his employers, 'especially when I pretended to fall down the stairs on my way out.'

Mr Ferro stayed in the job for 20 years, maintaining the pretence of his disability by bumping into doors and knocking things off desks. His deception was discovered when colleagues spotted his photo in the paper after he'd won a national cross-country roller-skating competition.

Australian Brandon Danvers received a prison sentence after he was caught speeding. An unusually harsh punishment? Not when you consider that at the time he was filming himself exceeding 100 mph. and masturbating at the wheel of his sports car, with a gun and a whole pile of drugs on the seat next to him.

John Ofosu, a 32-year-old from Ghana, regularly stole goats from nearby villages. He managed to escape detection until he was stopped one day by police sergeant Abel Kanawi, who was surprised at the number of people crammed in Ofosu's car. On closer examination, Ofosu's family actually consisted of 14 goats he had just stolen, dressed in clothes in order to disguise them.

The sergeant commented, 'I thought at first his wife and children were dreadfully deformed, but then I saw they were goats in Michael Jackson T-shirts, so I arrested him.'

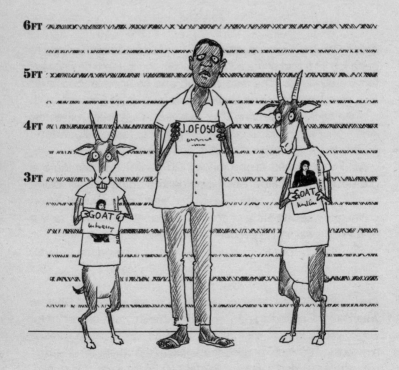

In 1998 the Nebraska Commission on Judicial Qualifications ousted a Douglas County Judge Richard 'Deacon' Jones, who admitted signing court papers 'Adolf Hitler' and 'Snow White' and tossing firecrackers in a colleague's office while shouting death threats. He was also accused of setting absurd bond amounts of 13 cents or a 'gazillion pengos' and swearing at court workers.

At his hearing Jones described some of his actions as pranks that went awry and said they did not violate any rules.

[FAIL]

In June 2012, 21-year-old Michael Ruse thought his two-week trial for assault was going well so he bragged to his friends on Facebook, 'I think I got away with it!' Ruse, who had denied beating up a friend's father, wrote his status update shortly before the jury was due to go out. The incriminating post was printed out and delivered anonymously to the court, where it was handed to the prosecution.

After being confronted by the new evidence Ruse had no choice but to change his plea to guilty. Judge Ian Pearson told Ruse, 'You pleaded guilty part-way through the trial only really because you were stupid enough to put on Facebook what amounted to a full confession. Your stupidity really is not much mitigation.'

Ruse was eventually sentenced to a 46-week prison sentence, suspended for two years, and put on a six-month curfew from 7 pm to 7 am. Russell Pyne, defending, said his client 'needs help with regards to thinking skills.'

Right-wing extremist Donald Leroy Evans, accused of murder in Fort Lauderdale, Florida, filed a motion before his trial for his name to be changed on all court papers to the name 'Hi Hitler'. Evans thought that Hitler's supporters had greeted their leader 'Hi, Hitler' rather than 'Heil, Hitler'.

A 38-stone Argentinian, Pablo de Casas, was always boasting about his incredible appetite. Challenged to a bet, he decided to put his money where his mouth was, and attempted to eat an 80lb-piglet. During the attempt his stomach stretched so much that he bled to death.

SEXUAL DISASTERS

> *'The problem with the gene pool is that there's no lifeguard.'*
>
> DAVID GERROLD

Whether it's an act with a partner or just self-gratification, when sex goes wrong, one of the most private acts in your life usually ends up with the most public consequences...

Some people want the greatest thrill, irrespective of the consequences, and such a case was reported in the *Japan Times* in April 1997. It recounted the story of a 13-year-old Thai boy called Charnchai Puanmuangpak, who was heavily into the craze known as 'pumping'. Participants insert a bicycle pump into their rectum so that the sudden rush of air creates a momentary high (don't try this at home).

Not content with the sensation, young Charnchai went a step too far. He and some friends went to a petrol station where he inserted an air line as far as he could. Almost as soon as he placed the coin into the slot to start the air he exploded.

The police commented, 'When that quantity of air interacted with the gas in his system it was like an atom bomb went off. We still haven't located all of him.'

A hospital spokesman who had witnessed a series of tragic pumping injuries commented, 'Pumping is the devil's pastime, and we must all say no to Satan. Inflate your tyres by all means, but then hide your bicycle pump where it cannot tempt you.'

In February 2001 a Taiwanese couple found a new angle for 'phone sex' when the man called his girlfriend on his Nokia 8850 mobile phone. Nothing unusual in that, you might think, except the phone was inserted in his girlfriend's bottom at the time. It seemed that the vibrating ring tone was very stimulating. The whole episode, however, ended in embarrassment when the phone slipped up inside the woman and couldn't be retrieved. After she experienced severe abdominal pains, the couple were forced to visit the Taipei Medical University Hospital, where it was eventually removed.

A Nokia spokesman commented, 'We can't control how the users use their phones. It's just a personal issue.'

There is such a thing as too much sex, as 28-year-old Russian Sergey Tuganov discovered after betting two women the equivalent of about £3,000 that he could continuously have sex with them both for 12 hours. Several minutes after winning the bet, he suffered a fatal heart attack, apparently due to having gulped down a whole bottle of Viagra to help his performance.

Twenty-year-old Karl Watkins appeared at Hereford Crown Court in 1993 on five counts of outraging public decency including 'making love to pavements'. He was seen face down with his pants around his ankles thrusting his hips up and down, surrounded by a group of curious children. Claiming a case of 'mistaken identity', Watkins received an 18-month jail sentence.

Police in Groningen, Holland, arrested a 25-year-old man and his 33-year-old lover for having sex on a car's bonnet. The car they were cavorting on was the police patrol car.

FAIL

It was after hours at the Condor, a club belonging to night-club boss and local gang leader Jimmy 'The Beard' Ferrozo – the perfect time for him and 23-year-old stripper Teresa Hill to have sex. And what better place than the club's grand piano?

As they writhed around on top of it Hill accidentally pressed the button that caused the piano to rise majestically up from the stage on a hydraulic lift. Caught in the heat of the moment, neither Hill nor Ferrozo noticed what was happening until it was too late and the piano hit the ceiling. The stripper got off lightly with just bruising but her boss was crushed to death.

In 2001 Andrew Farlow and his wife Rosemary were messing around in the bedroom when Andrew had the bright idea of spreading peanut butter around his crotch and seeing if the family dog would lick it off. It did more than that; in the excitement it sunk its teeth into his penis, too. That signalled the end of their sexual experimentation.

A video of a 1994 Sussex wedding reception had a few surprises for the guests who'd sat down to watch it afterwards with the happy couple. At the end of the video they saw 59-year-old Derek Jeffrey (the owner of the video camera) wearing nothing but his socks, taking part in unusual and unnatural acts with a Staffordshire bull terrler called Ronnie. He'd forgotten to erase the tape.

A man (who wished to remain nameless) who had a penile implant operation in Turkey discovered a drawback to the operation when he returned to his home on Merseyside. Since the two devices shared a common frequency, his implant is activated each time his neighbour used his remote control to open his garage door. According to the man, doctors would not help him because the alleged medical negligence happened in Turkey with equipment not recognized in the UK. Talking about his neighbour he commented, 'Every time his car pulls in, I can't leave the house.'

[FAIL]

When the Birmingham branch of Selfridges opened for business one morning in 2003, the last thing staff in the beds department expected to witness was a four-in-a-bed sex romp – particularly when three of the occupants were store mannequins. Aydin Demir had broken into the store during the night, removed the dummies and had gone to bed with them. He was charged with burglary and criminal damage.

A number of men in the US responded to an ad promoting what they thought was the bargain of the century: a penis enlarger for just $25. They were very disappointed when all they received was a magnifying glass.

In September 1999 Ron Guptey of New South Wales went to his local A&E department complaining of a severe pain in his rectum and a raging fever. Doctors were puzzled by the symptoms and admitted him to hospital where his condition soon worsened. He died the following day after lapsing into a coma. An autopsy revealed that a black widow spider had laid eggs in Ron's rectum. Once the baby spiders were hatched they had bitten him and had poisoned him from the inside. How did they get there? Well, the post-mortem also revealed traces of tree bark and KY jelly. Ron was apparently satisfying himself with a tree stump in his garden, but had obviously failed to notice the black widow nest.

In 1992 Darryl Washington and Maria Ramos were injured at New York's Bowery subway station when a train ran over them as they were having impromptu sex on a mattress they had thrown on to the tracks. Miraculously neither of them were seriously hurt. Recovering at Bellevue Hospital, Washington told reporters, 'I started kissing her. I closed my eyes, and the next thing I knew, something went "BANG!" It was a very big bang.' A shaken Ramos told detectives, 'Usually no trains run on that track.'

A 55-year-old man from Burbank, California, who was heavily into bondage met a like-minded soul and arranged to have a discipline session at his apartment. The 'date' duly arrived and according to his wishes, the man was stripped naked, spanked and then tightly tied to a 'discipline table' in his spare room. That's when the date's accomplice arrived and, with their victim bound and helpless, the two of them proceeded to steal his stereo, his new TV and his sofa.

Looking for a new sexual thrill, in 2007 31-year-old Gary Ashbrook from Newhaven, East Sussex, inflated a condom with laughing gas and put it over his head. He suffocated.

In November 2004, Nicolae Popovici, a 43-year-old Romanian father of five living in the town of Topraisar, decided he had enough children and was determined to avoid another pregnancy at any cost. When it turned out that the condoms his wife bought were too large, he decided on a practical solution rather than waste them: why not superglue the condom on to his penis? After sex he discovered the inevitable: the condom was stuck fast. After a dash to a nearby hospital, nursing staff worked for hours in an effort to remove it, which they eventually did.

(FAIL)

Police in Ohio were called to a house when a man reported his father lying face down on the couch, naked and not breathing. The man was pronounced dead and when he was removed, officers discovered two unusual sights: burn marks around his genitals and a small hole in one of the cushions in the position of his groin. Removing the cushion they found two electric sanders fixed to the couch frame.

It turned out that the man had a habit of putting his penis down the hole and enjoying the good vibrations of the sanders (with the sanding paper removed, of course). His death was caused by his orgasm shorting out one of the sanders, resulting in his electrocution.

SPORTING SLIP-UPS

> *'It is not enough to succeed; others must fail.'*
> GORE VIDAL

Huge errors of judgement, brawn over brains and just bad luck ... everything you need for induction into the Sporting Hall of Shame.

The Russian military rifle team arrived at the 1908 Olympics in London with due pomp and ceremony, only to discover that the tournament had taken place several days earlier. It turned out that the Russians were using the old Julian calendar while most other countries had adopted the Gregorian, which was 12 days shorter.

[FAIL]

In February 1995 the *Peterborough Evening Telegraph* was forced to declare its first 'Spot the Ball' competition null and void after the newspaper accidentally published the photograph with the ball still in it.

In 1995 a nine-foot-tall statue of legendary baseball star Babe Ruth was unveiled in front of Camden Yards Baseball Park, home of the Baltimore Orioles' professional baseball team.

The statue, by artist Susan Luery, depicted Ruth with a right-handed baseball glove. Ruth was left-handed.

[FAIL]

Keen runner John Oliver, 31, travelled over 5,000 miles from Bournemouth in Dorset to Nepal in order to take part in his first marathon, only to sprain his ankle on the starting line.

A non-league football match in Worthing was played with a minimum of stoppages after the referee accidentally dropped his whistle in cow dung at the edge of the pitch.

[FAIL]

In 1966 Colwyn Bay rugby club travelled 50 miles to play their Welsh rivals Portmadoc. Both teams faced each other for the kick-off when the referee noticed something was missing – the ball. Amazingly, no one could locate a spare ball so the game had to be abandoned.

Boxer Daniel Caruso had a strange way of preparing himself for a fight: he used to psyche himself up by punching himself in the face. Unfortunately, before the 1992 New York Golden Gloves championship, he went too far, breaking his own nose. Doctors examining him ruled that he was medically unfit to box.

Offering unlimited cheap beer to fans in order to attract them to a baseball game was probably not the brightest promotional idea – but that's exactly what the Cleveland Indians offered fans in order to attract a large crowd to their June 1974 game against the Texas Rangers. The offer attracted over 25,000 screaming fans to the game instead of the usual 8,000.

The baseball took second place in a scene reminiscent of the last days of the Roman Empire. Streakers ran amok, fighting broke out throughout the stadium, seats were ripped out, fans invaded the field while players were pelted with hot dogs, hamburger, beer – in fact, anything that wasn't bolted down. The Indians' manager ordered his players to use their bats to defend themselves against the drunken crowd and the riot squad was called out to restore order.

The umpire forfeited the game to Texas, describing the fans as 'uncontrollable beasts'.

[FAIL]

In 1994 Jeremy Brenno, a 16-year-old golfer from Gloverville, New York, was having a particularly bad game so he took it out on his club (a three wood), throwing it against a bench in a fit of rage. The shaft broke on impact and part of it bounced back, piercing his heart and killing him.

South Korean Kyong Soon-Yim finished last in the slalom in the 1960 Winter Olympics at Squaw Valley, California – but with good reason. He'd never actually skied on snow before in his life. Instead, Kyong Soon-Yim had read lots of books on the subject and watched other skiers on television to learn their techniques.

Seventeen-year-old Manuel Salgado, one of Brazil's most promising young boxers, suffered a serious setback to his career at a bout in Rio de Janeiro. Here, during an important fight, he was dragged from the ring by his mother, who wanted him to go home and finish his homework.

In 1975, furious viewers besieged WNBC-TV with complaints over a remark made by sports commentator Dick Schaap. He'd described racehorses Secretariat and Riva Ridge as 'the most famous pair of stablemates since Mary and Joseph'.

In October 1998 a football match in the Democratic Republic of Congo was stopped for a very unusual reason: one of the sides was struck by lightning. Players from Bena Tshadi were drawing 1–1 with home team rivals Basanga when a sudden freak lightning bolt wiped the whole team out, mid-game. The fact that players from Basanga escaped unharmed prompted accusations of witchcraft.

Champion Russian ice hockey goalkeeper Vladislav Tretiak had to retire from the 1981 USSR National Championships after fracturing his leg getting off a bus. He slipped on some ice.

FAIL

Turkish wrestler Youssouf Ishmaelo was immensely wealthy but because he didn't trust anyone to look after his money, he carried it everywhere he went in the form of gold ingots, carried inside a pouch worn round his waist. In 1898 he toured America with great success before returning to Turkey.

Unfortunately the boat on which he was travelling, the *Bourgoyne*, hit a reef and rapidly started to sink. All the passengers survived the wreck except Ishmaelo. The weight of the gold bullion around his waist prevented him from swimming to safety and he went down with the ship.

Four Turkish freestyle wrestlers who were due to compete at the 1952 Olympics in Helsinki were barred from competing. The Turkish sporting authority had forgotten to post their entries.

Coleridge Football Club in Cambridge couldn't wait for the 1984 edition of the *Guinness Book of Records* to come out. In it, they were going to be listed as the cleanest football team in the country. Since being formed in 1954, they hadn't had a single player booked. Unfortunately the weekend before the book was published they lost their clean sheet, having two players booked in the first 12 minutes of a game.

FAIL

In 1994 conker players Mark Tuckey and Martin Ashton were taking part in the Isle of Wight regional championship final when they set a new world record. After a hundred attempts they completely failed in hitting each other's conkers and the referee abandoned the match.

Organizers of the 1994 Waterlooville Festival mile-long fun run in Hampshire had high expectations for the race and a capacity field of entrants. Medals had been struck, marshals and timekeepers were ready and even a St John's Ambulance crew were standing by. A large crowd had gathered by the start of the race – all to see just one runner turn up, a seven-year-old schoolboy called Michael Biddell.

After the race a member of the festival committee commented, 'The medals did not have 1994 on them so we can use them again next year.'

FAIL

Not many people have heard of Formula One racing driver Marco Apicella. In the 1983 Italian Grand Prix he skidded off the track just before the first corner, having travelled only 800 metres. He decided never to race again.

At the 1982 North American Boxing Championships in Las Vegas the great Cuban heavyweight fighter Pedro Cardenas fought the Canadian Willie DeWitt. The match was halted in dramatic fashion in the first round when Cardenas swung a punch but missed and knocked out the referee Bert Lowes. A replacement referee was located and the round continued. Cardenas was nothing if not consistent and managed to miss DeWitt again, striking the second referee, also knocking him out cold.

The fight was stopped again and it was some time before a third referee could be found willing to step inside the ring. Eventually the fight restarted but Cardenas himself was KO'd – not by the referee in a revenge attack, but by his opponent.

The record for the fastest sending-off is held by Lee Todd, the Cross Farm Park Celtic striker who was sent off in a match against Taunton East Reach Wanderers in October 2000 after just two seconds. His offence? When the whistle was blown for kick-off, he muttered to the referee, 'Fuck me, that was loud!' – and was promptly shown the red card.

In 1988 Gloucestershire had to abandon its Sunday League cricket match against Swindon because the team's groundsman had got his cans mixed up – and sprayed weedkiller all over the pitch rather than fertilizer.

FAIL

At the 1972 Munich Olympics, American runners Rey Robinson and Eddie Hart were both strong contenders for the 100 metres. They both won their heats on the opening day of the games and went back to the Olympic Village for a rest until the quarter-finals that evening. About four o'clock, both men were watching TV when they saw athletes warming up for the 100-metre quarter-finals...

They raced round to the stadium by car but by the time they arrived, the race had been run. The US coach Stan Wright took full responsibility. He'd been using an old Olympic schedule that was 18 months out of date.

Meeting President Calvin Coolidge should have been one of the highlights of Chicago Bears football player Red Grange's life, but it turned into one of his most embarrassing moments instead. Senator McKinley of Illinois introduced him to the president, saying, 'Mr President, I'd like you to meet Red Grange, who plays with the Bears.' Coolidge shook Red's hand, said, 'Nice to meet you, young man. I've always liked animal acts' – and moved on.

FAIL

Keen athletes will practise anywhere, and none were keener than three Mozambique athletes competing in the 1991 World Student Games in Sheffield. They were delighted to find a nice stretch of straight road to run on which was close to their accommodation. Their practice sessions were soon brought to a halt, though, when they were arrested by police and charged with running on the M1 motorway.

Anglers Joan and William Parks thought they could outwit the locals in the annual Salmon Derby held in the Washington fishing town of Port Angeles. They managed to win first and second prizes but when challenged by suspicious rivals, their lack of attention to detail let them down; their prize-winning fish were found to be still partly frozen.

Former Manchester United goalkeeper Alex Stepney dislocated his jaw during a match in 1975. Not by making a courageous diving save and colliding with the goal post; he did it by shouting too much at his disorganized defence.

COMMENTATORS' COCK-UPS

'Success covers a multitude of blunders.'

GEORGE BERNARD SHAW

Whether you're a sports commentator or competitor, coach or manager offering your views before or after a game, it's easy to take your foot off the ball and put it straight in your mouth...

A reporter asked basketball star Michael Jordan how he felt being named one of the NBA's most reporter-friendly players. Jordan's reply was, 'No comment.'

'I came to Nantes two years ago and it's much the same today, except that it's completely different.'

COMMENTATOR BRIAN MOORE

'And he's got the ice pack on his groin there,
so it's possibly not the old shoulder injury.'

COMMENTATOR RAY FRENCH

'We knew Jermaine wasn't injured.
He was just hurt a little bit.'

BASKETBALL PLAYER RON ARTEST COMMENTING
ON A COLLEAGUE'S KNEE INJURY

'Gentlemen, I have nothing to say. Any questions?'

HOCKEY PLAYER PHIL WATSON AT A PRESS CONFERENCE

'Right now I have the three Cs: comfortable,
confident and seeing the ball well.'

BASEBALL PLAYER JAY BUHNER

'Sure there have been injuries and deaths in boxing –
but none of them serious.'

BOXER ALAN MINTER

'This fight is going to be 90 per cent mental and
50 per cent physical.'

BOXING MANAGER LOU DUVA

'Pitching is 80 per cent of the game.
The other half is hitting and fielding.'

BASEBALL PLAYER MICKEY RIVERS

FAIL

REPORTER: 'Is your improved play due to your maturity?'
HOCKEY PLAYER JAY MILLER: 'It's not so much maturity
as it is growing up.'

☹

'We're not as good as we think we are.
We need to go out there and prove that!'

FOOTBALL MANAGER STEVE MCCLAREN

FAIL

'Two questions – why were England so poor?
And if they were poor, why?'

COMMENTATOR IAN PAYNE COVERING THE WORLD CUP

☹

'If you make the right decision, it's normally
going to be the correct one.'

FOOTBALLER DAVE BEASANT

FAIL

'It's the millennium Wimbledon. There won't be another
millennium Wimbledon for another millennium.'

TENNIS PLAYER VENUS WILLIAMS

'You cannot change the stripes of a leopard.'

AMERICAN FOOTBALL PLAYER EMMITT SMITH

REPORTER: 'Will your injury keep you out for six weeks?'
BASEBALL PLAYER JUNIOR ORTIZ: 'No, longer than that.
Maybe a month and a half.'

FAIL

'They're the second best team in the world and there's no
higher praise than that.'

FOOTBALLER AND MANAGER KEVIN KEEGAN

'I owe a lot to my parents, especially my mother and father.'

GOLFER GREG NORMAN

US basketball star Shaquille O'Neal was asked by a journalist if he had visited the Parthenon during a trip to Greece. He replied, 'I can't really remember the names of all the clubs we went to.'

'We've got a good squad and we're going to cut our cloth accordingly. But I think the cloth we've got could make some good soup, if that makes any sense.'

FOOTBALL MANAGER IAN HOLLOWAY

'We're a long way from being where we are.'

FOOTBALLER STEVEN GERRARD

'It's gold or nothing – and it's nothing! He comes away with a silver medal.'

BROADCASTER DAVID COLEMAN

'We had four must-win games and we musted.'

BASEBALL PITCHER CURT SCHILLING

'Watch the expression on his mask.'

ICE HOCKEY COMMENTATOR HARRY NEALE

'I've never been so certain about anything in my life. I want to be a coach or a manager; I'm not sure which.'

FOOTBALLER PHIL NEVILLE

'In a sense it's a one-man show ... except there are two men involved, Hartson and Berkovic, and third man, the goalkeeper.'

COMMENTATOR JOHN MOTSON

'One of the great unknown champions because very little is known about him.'

BROADCASTER DAVID COLEMAN

'We lost because we didn't win.'

FOOTBALLER CRISTIANO RONALDO

'There's bound to be a deeply beating heart inside that young brain.'

COMMENTATOR BILL LESLIE

'I can see the carrot at the end of the tunnel.'

FOOTBALLER STUART PEARCE

'There are two ways of getting the ball – one way is from your own players, and that's the only way.'

FOOTBALL MANAGER TERRY VENABLES

'And here's Moses Kiptanui, the 19-year-old Kenyan, who turned 20 a few weeks ago.'

BROADCASTER DAVID COLEMAN

'We talked five times. I called him twice and
he called me twice.'

BASEBALL MANAGER LARRY BOWA

☹

JIMMY HILL: 'But you said it should have been a goal.'
TERRY VENABLES: 'No, I didn't. I said it should have been a
goal.'
JIMMY HILL: 'So you've changed your tune, then.'

FAIL

A complete motorsports enthusiast, Murray Walker
commentated on Formula One racing from 1949 right up until
his retirement in 2001 and is best known for sometimes
getting extremely over-excited in the heat of the moment,
leading to some very entertaining comments...

• 'He's obviously gone in for a wheel change. I say obviously
  because I can't see it.'

• 'With half the race gone, there is half the race still to go.'

• 'And now, excuse me while I interrupt myself.'

• 'And that just shows you how important the car is in
  Formula One Racing.'

• 'Either the car is stationary, or it's on the move.'

• 'He can't decide whether to leave his visor half-open or
  half-closed.'

• 'That's history. I say history because it happened in
  the past.'

- 'The lead car is unique, except for the one behind it, which is identical.'

- '...and Edson Arantes do Nascimento, commonly known as Pelé, hands his award to Damon Hill, commonly known as, uh, uh, Damon Hill.'

- 'There's nothing wrong with the car except that it is on fire.'

- 'Tambay's hopes, which were nil before, are absolutely zero now.'

GAME SHOW GAFFES

> *'All the world loves a good loser.'*
> KIN HUBBARD

Not so much **The Weakest Link** *as the Missing Link...*
When it comes to making fools of themselves by
giving truly idiotic answers, TV and radio game show
contestants have their fingers firmly on the button.

FAIL

HOST: 'Who killed Cock Robin?'
CONTESTANT: 'Oh, God. I didn't even know he was dead!'

(AUSTRALIAN GAME SHOW THE AFTERNOON PROGRAMME QUIZ)

HOST: 'What "W" is Ronald Reagan's middle name?'
CONTESTANT: 'Wepublican.'

(BLOCKBUSTERS)

FAIL

HOST: 'After a 76-year absence, what comet last appeared in 1986?'
CONTESTANT: 'Spider-Man.'

(BINGO AMERICA)

DJ: 'What creature squirts a smelly unpleasant fluid at its enemies?'
CONTESTANT: 'A snake.'
DJ: 'No, I'll give you a clue – it's black and white.'
CONTESTANT: 'A bee.'

(CAPITAL RADIO COMPETITION)

FAIL

DJ: 'Who wrote *Hamlet*?'
CONTESTANT: 'Um ... Macbeth.'

(CAPITAL GOLD RADIO COMPETITION)

DJ: 'What is the nationality of the Pope?'
CONTESTANT: 'I think I know that one. Is it Jewish?'

(US RADIO PHONE-IN COMPETITION)

FAIL

GAME SHOW HOST: 'Which mathematician said, "The most incomprehensible thing about the universe is that it's comprehensible"?'
CONTESTANT: 'Mel Gibson.'

(2BL 702 RADIO SHOW, AUSTRALIA)

HOST: 'Name a prime number between 20 and 40.'
CONTESTANT: 'Between 20 and 40?'
HOST: 'Yes.'
CONTESTANT: 'Seven.'

(WINTUITION GAME SHOW)

HOST: 'Where does Dracula come from?'
CONTESTANT: 'Umm ... Pennsylvania.'

(QUIZ SEGMENT ON VIRGIN RADIO BREAKFAST SHOW)

Real answers from *Family Fortunes*, or the American equivalent *Family Feuds*:

Q: Something Russia is famous for...
A: Russians.

Q: Something red...
A: My cardigan.

Q: Something a blind person might use...
A: A sword.

Q: A song with 'Moon' in the title...
A: Blue Suede Moon.

Q: An animal you might see at a zoo...
Q: A dog.

Q: A famous bridge...
A: Bridge Over Troubled Waters.

Q: An item of clothing worn by the Three Musketeers…
A: A horse.

Q: A famous royal…
A: Mail.

Q: Something made of wool…
A: Sheep.

Q: A word that a dog understands…
A: Ruff.

Q: Something you open other than a door...
A: Your bowels.

Q: Something you do in the bathroom...
A: Decorate.

Q: Something that floats in the bath...
A: Water.

Q: A romantic-sounding musical instrument...
A: Drum.

Q: A famous Arthur...
A: Shakespeare.

Q: A bird with a long neck...
A: Naomi Campbell.

Q: Something people might be allergic to...
A: Skiing.

Q: Something you might accidentally leave on all night...
A: Your shoe.

Q: An invention that had replaced stairs...
A: The wheel.

Q: Something a cat can do...
A: Go to the toilet.

Q: A number you need to memorize...
A: Seven.

Q: Something you might wear on the beach...
A: Deckchair.

Q: A domestic animal...
A: Leopard.

Q: Something that would annoy a gardener...
A: Not being paid on time.

Q: What should you drink a lot of when you're sick...
A: Alcohol.

Q: A way of cooking fish...
A: Cod.

Q: Something you squeeze...
A: Peanut butter.

Q: A fruit that is yellow...
A: Orange.

Q: Something you'd find in a birdcage...
A: A hamster.

Q: An animal with three letters in its name...
A: Alligator.

Q: Something that flies that doesn't have an engine...
A: A bicycle with wings.

☹

Real answers from *The Weakest Link*:

HOST: Which surname is shared by a real cowboy called Butch and a fictional one called Hopalong?
CONTESTANT: Lesbian.

HOST: The term 'Rubenesque' derives from which seventeenth-century artist?
CONTESTANT: Aretha Franklin.

HOST: In Tolkien's *Lord of the Rings* trilogy, the third and final book is called *The Return of the...* what?
CONTESTANT: Jedi.

HOST: Which character narrates all but four of the Sherlock Holmes books?
CONTESTANT: The Pink Panther.

HOST: The four gospels of the New Testament are attributed to Matthew, Mark, Luke and who?
CONTESTANT: Joe.

HOST: Which letter of the alphabet sounds exactly the same as the term for a female sheep?
CONTESTANT: Baa.

HOST: Who wrote *Cat on a Hot Tin Roof*?
CONTESTANT: Dr Seuss.

HOST: A book about the stereotype of male masculinity is entitled *Real Men Don't Eat...* what?
CONTESTANT: Food.

HOST: What word, meaning devil, is an anagram of the word 'Santa'?
CONTESTANT: Anstas.

HOST: What was the principal language used by the ancient Romans?
CONTESTANT: Greek.

HOST: In *Rupert Bear* the character called Edward Trunk is a representation of which animal?
CONTESTANT: Weasel.

HOST: The M4 motorway toll bridge in the UK crosses which river?
CONTESTANT: The Seine.

HOST: Sudan is the largest country in which continent?
CONTESTANT: Europe.

HOST: According to the proverb, a new broom sweeps what?
CONTESTANT: Old dust.

HOST: The cockney rhyming slang for road is 'Frog and...' what?
CONTESTANT: Pears.

HOST: The ancient site known as the Valley of the Kings is in which country?
CONTESTANT: England.

HOST: What do tigers have, spots or stripes?
CONTESTANT: A tiger.

HOST: Which popular hot drink is an anagram of the word 'eat'?
CONTESTANT: Chocolate.

HOST: What is the highest double-figured number?
CONTESTANT: Twenty-five.

HOST: In the film *Deliverance*, a scene involves a duo between stringed instruments – a guitar and what?
CONTESTANT: Cello.

HOST: Cognac is a fine brandy made from the juice of which fruit?
CONTESTANT: Coconut.

HOST: What is the name of the insect which makes honey?
CONTESTANT: Honey Fly.

HOST: A clog is worn on which part of the body?
CONTESTANT: The bottom.

HOST: What is the three-letter name of the area which is the background for the sun, moon and stars?
CONTESTANT: Sea.

HOST: The word 'ape' is an anagram of which small vegetable?
CONTESTANT: Apple.

HOST: *The Tale of Two Cities* starts: 'It was the best of times, it was...' what?
CONTESTANT: Summer.

HOST: What 'K' is the currency of Sweden?
CONTESTANT: Kennel.

HOST: What is the highest prime number under ten?
CONTESTANT: Eleven.

HOST: The equator divides the world into how
many hemispheres?
CONTESTANT: Three.

HOST: What does a bat use to facilitate flying in the dark?
CONTESTANT: Wings.

HOST: What 'Z' is used to describe a human who has
returned from the dead?
CONTESTANT: Unicorn.

HOST: In traffic, what 'J' is where two roads meet?
CONTESTANT: Jool carriageway.

FAIL

CELEBRITIES SAY AND DO THE DUMBEST THINGS

> 'Success is often achieved by those who don't know that failure is inevitable.'
>
> COCO CHANEL

There are celebrities who take advantage of their position on the world stage to make a difference, making inspirational, campaigning pronouncements. Then there are those with nice hair...

INTERVIEWER: 'Are you attending the Cannes Film Festival?'
CHRISTINA AGUILERA: 'I hope so. Where is it being held this year?'

'I hate it when women wear the wrong foundation colour. It might be the worst thing on the planet when they wear their make-up too light.'

KIM KARDASHIAN

'I've got ten pairs of trainers.
That's one for every day of the week.'

SAMANTHA FOX

SINGER TAYLOR HANSON DURING A 'MEET THE FANS'
EVENT: 'What day of the week is it?'
FAN: 'Friday.'
HANSON: 'All day?'

REPORTER: 'Why do you think you've been reincarnated?'
LEE RYAN (OF BOY BAND BLUE): 'Every time I eat
chicken I eat it with my hands – like they did in the
olden days.'

'Fiction writing is great, you can make up almost anything.'

IVANA TRUMP, ON FINISHING HER FIRST NOVEL

FAIL

'I don't think having a naked woman strapped to a
rack is sexist at all. And I don't think the fact that
we pretend to slit her throat is violent.'

BLACKIE LAWLESS OF ROCK GROUP W.A.S.P.

'We were young and sacrificed a lot.
I had to give up cheerleading.'

BEYONCÉ KNOWLES TALKING ABOUT
FORMING DESTINY'S CHILD

REPORTER: 'Britney, how do you feel about the meeting
between George Bush and Tony Blair this week?'
BRITNEY SPEARS: 'Who's Tony Blair?'
REPORTER: 'He's the prime minister of Britain.'
BRITNEY SPEARS: 'Well, he must be a very important
person.'

'Smoking kills. If you're killed you've lost
a very important part of your life.'

BROOKE SHIELDS
(AS SPOKESPERSON FOR A US ANTI-SMOKING CAMPAIGN)

'I mean, part of the beauty of me is that I'm very rich.'

DONALD TRUMP

'I'm a bitchin' rock star from Mars.'

CHARLIE SHEEN

'I got to a lot of overseas places, like Canada.'

BRITNEY SPEARS

'I'm not anorexic. I'm from Texas.'

JESSICA SIMPSON

'Eskimos are uncivilized because they
don't have any shops.'

JODIE MARSH

'Whenever I watch TV and see those poor starving
kids all over the world, I can't help but cry. I mean
I'd love to be skinny like that but not with all those
flies and death and stuff.'

MARIAH CAREY

'Oh dear. Who was she?'

JOAN CRAWFORD ON 7 DECEMBER 1941 AFTER BEING TOLD
'THE JAPANESE HAVE ATTACKED PEARL HARBOR'

'How did you guys run so slowly in that opening *Baywatch* scene – you know, where you were running down to the beach?'

JESSICA SIMPSON TO PAMELA ANDERSON

FAIL

'Doesn't that hurt?'

ANNA NICOLE SMITH, AFTER SHE WAS
TOLD ABOUT SUICIDE BOMBERS

☹

'What's Walmart? Do they sell, like, wall stuff?'

PARIS HILTON

FAIL

'When I get lonely, I want to be alone. I like to indulge in my loneliness so I can figure out that I'm not really lonely.'

ALICIA SILVERSTONE

☹

'I was asked to come to Chicago because Chicago is one of our 52 states.'

RAQUEL WELCH

FAIL

'I think it is really important people eat.'

TARA REID

'It's important to be thankful, even if you're poor.
I mean, come on, we all have clean water – well, OK,
not people in the developing world.'

AVRIL LAVIGNE

'I never really wanted to go to Japan simply because
I don't really like eating fish. I know that's very popular
out there in Africa.'

BRITNEY SPEARS

[FAIL]

'You can hardly tell where the computer models finish
and the real dinosaurs begin.'

LAURA DERN ON *JURASSIC PARK*

'In an action film you act in the action. If it's a dramatic
film you act in the drama.'

JEAN-CLAUDE VAN DAMME

[FAIL]

'[Starring as Joan of Arc] was incredibly trying on a
physical level, but what kept me going was the thought
that no matter how difficult it was for me, I knew it had
been a lifetime more difficult for Joan.'

MILLA JOVOVICH

'I went in and said, "If I see one more gratuitous shot of a woman's body I'm quitting." I think the show should be emotional story lines, morals, real-life heroes. And that's what we're doing.'

DAVID HASSELHOFF, REFERRING TO BAYWATCH

'I'm sincere. I'm really curious. I care what people think. I listen to answers and I leave my ego at the door. I don't use the word "I".'

LARRY KING

'I feel at my best when I'm happy.'

WINONA RYDER

'Why do people treat me with fun just because I am the biggest, strongest and most beautiful man in the world?'

ARNOLD SCHWARZENEGGER

FAIL

'People all over the world recognize me as a spiritual leader.'

ACTION STAR STEVEN SEAGAL

'God's, like, so cool. Think of the coolest person in our life. He made that person. And he's cooler than that.'

JUSTINE BATEMAN

FAIL

'Twenty-three is old. It's almost twenty-five, which is, like, almost mid-twenties.'

JESSICA SIMPSON

'I want only two houses, rather than seven. I feel like letting go of things.'

BARBRA STREISAND

FAIL

ROLLING STONE MAGAZINE: 'What's the best thing you read all year?'
JUSTIN TIMBERLAKE: 'You mean like a book?'

Actress Tori Spelling was asked by radio host Howard Stern if she knew the capital of New York. 'Of course,' she replied. 'New Jersey.'

'I haven't read a book in my life. I haven't got enough time. I do love fashion magazines.'

VICTORIA BECKHAM

'I'm not a fan of books. I would never want a book's autograph.'

KANYE WEST

'I still feel alone, because no one – including me – understands my mind.'

R. KELLY

'It was God who made me so beautiful. If I weren't, then I'd be a teacher.'

LINDA EVANGELISTA

'It's really hard to maintain a one-on-one relationship if the other person is not going to allow me to be with other people.'

AXL ROSE

THEY TURNED IT DOWN

> *'If you're gonna fail, fail big ...'*
> DENZEL WASHINGTON

You're offered the starring role in a great movie with the full backing of the studio. What's not to like? The following actors were offered lead roles in some of the top-grossing films of all time, but for various reasons, they actually decided to turn them down...

Movie star	Hit film they turned down starring role in	Who took the role
Julia Roberts	*Sleepless in Seattle*	Meg Ryan
	Shakespeare in Love	Gwyneth Paltrow
	Basic Instinct	Sharon Stone
David Schwimmer	*Men in Black*	Will Smith
Sean Connery	*The Matrix*	Laurence Fishburne
	Lord of the Rings	Sir Ian McKellen

Movie star	Hit film they turned down starring role in	Who took the role
Will Smith	*The Matrix*	Keanu Reeves
Tom Hanks	*Field of Dreams*	Kevin Costner
	Shawshank Redemption	Tim Robbins
	Jerry Maguire	Tom Cruise
Warren Beatty	*The Sting*	Robert Redford
	Wall Street	Michael Douglas
	The Graduate	Dustin Hoffman
Mel Gibson	*The Terminator*	Arnold Schwarzenegger
	Batman	Michael Keaton
Al Pacino	*Close Encounters of the Third Kind*	Richard Dreyfuss
	Midnight Cowboy	Dustin Hoffman
	Kramer vs Kramer	Dustin Hoffman
	Marathon Man	Dustin Hoffman
	Star Wars	Harrison Ford
Gregory Peck	*Cape Fear*	Robert Mitchum
	High Noon	Gary Cooper
Harrison Ford	*Alien*	Tom Skerritt
	Big	Tom Hanks
	The Hunt for Red October	Alec Baldwin
	Jurassic Park	Sam Neill
	Misery	James Caan
	The Perfect Storm	George Clooney
	Schindler's List	Liam Neeson

Movie star	Hit film they turned down starring role in	Who took the role
Johnny Depp	*Thelma and Louise*	Brad Pitt
	X-Men	Hugh Jackman
Jack Nicholson	*Apocalypse Now*	Martin Sheen
	Bruce Almighty	Morgan Freeman
	The Godfather	Al Pacino
	Rain Man	Dustin Hoffman
	Taxi Driver	Robert De Niro
Kim Basinger	*Basic Instinct*	Sharon Stone
	Ghost	Demi Moore
	Sleepless In Seattle	Meg Ryan
	Speed	Sandra Bullock
Marlon Brando	*High Noon*	Gary Cooper
Jodie Foster	*Scarface*	Michelle Pfeiffer
	Manhattan	Mariel Hemingway
	Sleepless in Seattle	Meg Ryan
Dustin Hoffman	*Superman*	Gene Hackman
	The Godfather	Al Pacino
	Misery	James Caan
	Who Framed Roger Rabbit?	Bob Hoskins
	Blade Runner	Harrison Ford
Anthony Hopkins	*Gandhi*	Ben Kingsley
Jeff Bridges	*Raiders of the Lost Ark*	Harrison Ford
Paul Newman	*Romancing the Stone*	Michael Douglas
	Signs	Mel Gibson
	Terms of Endearment	Jack Nicholson

Movie star	Hit film they turned down starring role in	Who took the role
Audrey Hepburn	*The Sound of Music*	Julie Andrews
Clint Eastwood	*Superman*	Christopher Reeve
Elvis Presley	*Midnight Cowboy*	John Voight
	A Star Is Born	Kris Kristofferson
Cary Grant	*Dr. No*	Sean Connery
Steve McQueen	*Butch Cassidy & the Sundance Kid*	Robert Redford
	The French Connection	Gene Hackman
	Apocalypse Now	Martin Sheen

THAT'S ENTERTAINMENT?

> *'My reputation grows with every failure.'*
> GEORGE BERNARD SHAW

Mass entertainment is said to be consumed like fast food. That's quite appropriate since it can leave you bloated and disappointed with a bad taste in your mouth...

FAIL

Considered by many to be the worst circus in the world, Bob's Circus toured the American Midwest throughout the 1950s. Among the exhibits gracing its big top (which was ripped so spectators got soaked during rain showers) were a 'Stripeless Zebra' that was in reality just a large dog, while the daring animal trainers were actually children or dwarfs in cages with house cats (small trainers were used to make the 'jungle cats' look larger). There was also a 'Bearded Man' – although why this was a rare exhibit was never explained, and the beard was fake anyway.

To add insult to injury, there was also a touring Bob's Circus Lite that appeared in towns that were too small for the main circus. This was just a tent containing photographs of the various acts.

When *The Sound of Music* was released in South Korea, it turned out to be too long for local audiences' tastes. In order to make it more acceptable the local distributor decided to make a few cuts. He removed all the songs.

FAIL

In April 2004 in what was supposed to be one of the most exciting moments on the TV show *Ripley's Believe It Or Not!*, a one-ton ball made entirely of rubber bands nearly 15 feet across was dropped out of an aircraft a mile above the Mojave Desert in Arizona while a skydiving cameraman filmed its descent. The ball, which reached a speed of up to 400 mph, was expected to bounce over 100 feet into the air. However, after its 20-second descent, it hit the ground and broke apart on impact.

The lowest-grossing film in history is recognized to be the 2006 American indie film *Zyzzyx Road*, from director John Penney. A thriller with a reasonable cast, including Tom Sizemore and Katherine Heigl, the movie took 20 days to film and although it had a limited release, grossed just $30 at the box office from just six patrons – although $10 was refunded to the film's make-up artist who paid to see it.

FAIL

The last gunfight in the 1969 western *Butch Cassidy and the Sundance Kid* featured Robert Redford firing two six-shooters. Amazingly he managed to fire 17 shots without reloading.

A Parable of the Blind was a show put on at the Edinburgh Festival in 1988 by the ironically named Empty Space Theatre Company. Despite a considerable number of complimentary tickets being handed out in order to boost the attendance, not one person turned up to see the show, billed as 'Blind, blissful, medieval figures dance towards Brueghel's inevitable ditch, while in a mythical East, goldfish have their eyes plucked out in order to sing better.'

[FAIL]

Polish filmmaker Zbigniew Rybczyński was overjoyed after winning the Oscar for the Best Animated Short Film for *Tango* in 1982. After collecting his award, Rybczyński stepped outside for a cigarette but was unable to return to the awards ceremony after a security guard interpreted his thick accent as slurred speech, assumed he was a drunk, and refused to let him back in.

Rybczyński reportedly yelled, 'American Pig! I have Oscar!' and tried to kick the guard in the groin. He missed the rest of the Oscars after spending the night in jail.

The 1968 movie *Krakatoa: East of Java* is about the 1883 eruption of the volcanic island named in the title. Geography wasn't a strong subject for the filmmakers. Krakatoa actually lies west of Java.

Professor Marvo, an Argentinian magician, failed to live up to his name while performing his trick of catching a bullet in his teeth. What should have happened was that his assistant would fire a blank and he would produce a bullet that he had cleverly concealed in his mouth. Unfortunately, in one performance in 1988 an excited audience member, Marco Asprella, couldn't wait for the trick to start so he took out his own .45-calibre handgun and shot it at the magician, yelling, 'Catch this one, Professor!' – with predictable results.

During his subsequent trial for murder, Asprella made it clear that he couldn't understand why Professor Marvo hadn't caught the bullet as he promised. The jury sympathized and he was instead found guilty of carrying a concealed weapon for which he received a small fine.

[FAIL]

Austrian dwarf and circus acrobat Franz Dasch was at the top of his game when he performed at an event in northern Thailand in July 1999. He executed a perfect bounce from a trampoline, landing in the mouth of a yawning hippo. The animal was thought to have suffered a gag reflex, resulting in Dasch being swallowed whole. The 7,000-strong audience got to their feet and applauded, assuming this was part of the act. It wasn't.

In 1979 the budget for the western *Heaven's Gate*, a film without any major stars or special effects, escalated from $11.6 million (£7.25 million) to a record (at the time) $45 million (£28.1 million). Fifteen times more footage was shot by director Michael Cimino than was normal for that sort of film, which ended up as a three hour 39 minute epic. United Artists edited it down to two hours 29 minutes but even this couldn't save it. Universally panned by critics, it earned a paltry $3 million (£1.9 million), which caused the collapse of the studio and destroyed the reputation of the director. When asked by *People* magazine how *Heaven's Gate* had affected his life, Cimino said, 'Since then, I've been unable to make any movie that I've wanted to make. I've been making the best of what is available.'

My Mother the Car was named by *TV Guide* as the worst sitcom of all time. The show aired on NBC in September 1965 and involved the dead mother of character Dave Crabtree communicating with her son through his car radio (he was the only person who could hear her). Plots were as outlandish as the premise itself: in one episode his mother manages to prevent the planned assassination of a foreign leader. Critics say the show made light of what might be considered mental illness. The show was cancelled after a year.

[FAIL]

Think *Glee* but set in a police precinct, *Cop Rock* tried to combine the grittiest and most realistic TV genre with the most unrealistic – the musical. Devised by Steve Bocho, the man behind the critically acclaimed shows *Hill Street Blues* and *LA Law*, it was the most expensive television show at the time (September 1990) and relied on viewers not finding it odd that police would break into song and dance after they arrest a criminal, or a jury would do likewise just to announce the verdict. Bocho ignored ABC's requests to drop the musical numbers from the show and it was cancelled after three months, gaining infamy as one of the biggest television failures of the 1990s.

The Crusades was a 1935 movie directed by Cecil B. DeMille which showed the world between 1189 and 1199. In one scene Richard the Lionheart pulls back his cloak to check his watch.

According to the *British Medical Journal*, in November 2005 a Canadian sword-swallower died after attempting a variation of his act by swallowing an umbrella. When it was down his throat he accidentally pushed the button that opened it.

☹

The Altmark Theatre in the East German town of Stendal received a deluge of complaints after its 2004 Christmas production of *Snow White*. Theatregoers were disappointed that there were only four dwarfs, but the theatre spokesman explained that this was due to budgetary constraints.

(FAIL)

No matter where she looked or who she asked, British soul singer Lena Fiagbe couldn't find the Radio One Roadshow in Bangor. Eventually she discovered that instead of being in Bangor, North Wales, she should have been in Bangor, Northern Ireland. Ironically she missed her chance to perform her 1993 top-20 single, 'Gotta Get It Right'.

It was March 1998 and children in the packed Connaught Cinema in Worthing were looking forward to watching *Rainbow*, a 1996 family film starring Bob Hoskins, about a group of children and their dog who travel along a magical rainbow. Waiting expectedly in their seats they were soon faced with what one angry parent described as 'lesbian lovemaking, effing and blinding and full-frontal nudity'.

The projectionist had actually put on Ken Russell's *The Rainbow*, based on a sexually explicit novel by D. H. Lawrence.

(FAIL)

It was with high expectations that *Oscar Wilde: The Musical* opened at the Shaw Theatre in London in October 2004 to commemorate the 150th anniversary of Wilde's birth. Written by ex-Radio One DJ Mike Read, it ran for just one performance, closing after being universally panned. The *Daily Telegraph* said it was 'hard to feel anything other than incredulous contempt'. The *Guardian* was equally scathing, commenting on technical issues: 'You begin to wonder whether the sound system is being affected by the hefty rumbling of Oscar Wilde turning in his grave.'

☹

The world premiere of Walt Disney's *Pinocchio* took place in New York in February 1940. Walt himself had the idea of hiring 11 midgets, dressing them up as the puppet and putting them on top of Radio City Music Hall so they could wave hello to children entering the theatre. In a moment of madness, wine was sent up with their lunch and by the middle of the hot afternoon, there were 11 drunken naked midgets running around on top of the roof, belching and screaming obscenities at the crowd below.

They were removed by police who carried them away in pillowcases.

FAIL

In his day, studio boss Sam Goldwyn (the 'G' in MGM) was one of the richest men in Hollywood. Not bad for a barely educated, ex-glove salesman from Minsk originally called Samuel Goldfish. Unfortunately he was also famous for his meanness, his lack of tact and his unique ability to mangle the English language. A number of famous 'Goldwynisms' have now passed into legend. They include:

- 'I don't want any yes men around me. I want everyone to tell me the truth – even if it costs them their jobs!'

- 'Why call him Joe? Every Tom, Dick and Harry is called Joe!'

- 'It's more than magnificent – it's mediocre!'

- 'Let's have some new clichés!'

- 'I'll give you a definite maybe.'

- 'He's living beyond his means – but he can afford it.'

- 'I had a great idea this morning, but I didn't like it.'

- 'A verbal contract's not worth the paper it's written on.'

- 'You've bitten the hand of the goose that laid the golden egg.'

- 'Include me out.'

- 'Anyone who has to see a psychiatrist needs his head examined.'

- 'In two words, 'Im Possible'.'

- 'What we want is a story that starts with an earthquake and works its way up to a climax.'

THEY CALLED IT WRONG

'All you need in this life is ignorance and confidence, and then success is sure.'

MARK TWAIN

When it comes to making pronouncements, some of the world's best minds have made some of the worst errors of judgement...

[FAIL]

A Universal Pictures executive rejected not just one but two future stars at the same time, saying, 'Mr Reynolds, you have no talent. Mr Eastwood, your Adam's apple sticks out too far and you talk too slow.' Burt and Clint didn't let this little bit of criticism affect them too much.

'It will be gone by June.'

VARIETY MAGAZINE COMMENTING ON
THE FAD OF ROCK 'N' ROLL IN 1955

[FAIL]

'I'm going to live to be 100.'

AMERICAN HEALTH EXPERT AND AUTHOR JEROME RODALE
IN 1971. HE DIED THE NEXT DAY AGED FIFTY-ONE

[FAIL]

'The wireless music box has no imaginable commercial value.
Who would pay for a message sent to nobody in particular?'

RESPONSE FROM THE ASSOCIATES OF RCA FOUNDER DAVID
SARNOFF IN THE 1920s, WHEN HE PROPOSED INVESTING IN THE
FLEDGLING RADIO INDUSTRY.

In 1960 Thomas Monaghan and his brother James borrowed
$900 (£560) and bought and ran a failed pizza parlour in
Ypsilanti, Michigan. A year later James decided to sell his
half-share in the business for his brother's second-hand
Volkswagen Beetle. Thomas soldiered on and in 1965 he
renamed the pizza company Domino's Pizza. In 1998 he sold
93 per cent of the business for an estimated $1 billion
(£0.62 billion). What became of the VW Beetle is unknown...

[FAIL]

In 1966, while studying at Yale University, a student named
Fred Smith put forward an idea for a reliable overnight delivery
service in one of his assignments. His professor commented
that 'the concept is interesting and well-formed but in order to
earn better than a "C", the idea must be feasible'. Despite his
tutor's comments, five years later Smith turned his idea into
reality and formed Federal Express, which today has revenues
of almost $40 billion (£25 billion).

Dick Rowe, an A&R man working for Decca Records, was reportedly responsible for turning down The Beatles after they auditioned in January 1962. He supposedly told manager Brian Epstein, 'I'm sorry, but guitar groups are on their way out.'

☹

In 1903 Henry Ford's lawyer, Horace Rackham, was discussing his client with the president of the Michigan Savings Bank, whose sage advice was not to invest in the new venture, claiming, 'The horse is here to stay but the automobile is only a novelty – a fad.'

FAIL

Tony Faddell designed a small, hard disk-based music player that could be loaded with music through a simple content-delivery system. In 2000 he approached US company RealNetworks and also Philips but they both passed on his idea. He then took it to Apple.

You may have heard of the iPod and iTunes.

☹

'We are probably nearing the limit of all we can know about astronomy.'

SIMON NEWCOMB, CANADIAN-BORN
AMERICAN ASTRONOMER, 1888

FAIL

When a senior NBC executive saw the first episodes of *Star Trek* in 1966 he gave creator Gene Roddenberry a little piece of advice that would improve the show: 'Get rid of the pointed-ears guy.'

In the 31 October 1977 issue of *New York* magazine, business journalist Bill Flanagan predicted that *Close Encounters of the Third Kind* would be a 'colossal flop', and that the film 'lacks dazzle, charm, wit and imagination'. The film cost about $18 million (£11.2 million) to shoot and grossed almost $290 million (£181 million), making it at the time Columbia Pictures' most profitable film ever.

'I'll be damned if I'll spend two years of my life out in the desert on some fucking camel.'

MARLON BRANDO IN 1962, TURNING DOWN THE STARRING ROLE IN LAWRENCE OF ARABIA, A PART TAKEN BY AN UNKNOWN PETER O'TOOLE, WHO WON AN OSCAR NOMINATION FOR HIS PERFORMANCE

While at school in Port Huron, Michigan, third-grader Thomas Edison was diagnosed with having mental retardation and was expelled. He went on to perfect the light bulb and invent the phonograph and the movie projector.

The American author Jim Fixx pioneered better health through jogging and turned the whole craze into an industry in the 1970s. He wrote the best-selling *The Complete Book of Running* in 1977 and prided himself on being able to run ten miles each day, claiming, 'Research has shown that with endurance training such as running, the heart becomes a distinctly more efficient instrument.'

He died in July 1984 from a massive heart attack while out jogging.

King William I of Prussia was convinced that trains had no future in his empire. In 1884 he declared: 'No one will pay good money to get from Berlin to Potsdam in one hour when he can ride his horse there in one day for free.'

[FAIL]

'A cookie store is a bad idea. Besides, the market research reports say America likes crispy cookies, not soft and chewy cookies like you make.' This was just one of the many rejections Debbi Fields received for her new business idea. This didn't stop her opening her first shop in 1977. Now Mrs Fields' Cookies has nearly 400 locations throughout the US.

'The United States will not be a threat to us for decades.'

ADOLF HITLER, NOVEMBER 1940

[FAIL]

When Microsoft CEO Steve Ballmer got it wrong, he got it wrong big time. Talking about Google he said, 'Google's not a real company. It's a house of cards.' He also didn't have much faith about Apple's iPhone, claiming: 'There's no chance that the iPhone is going to get any significant market share. No chance.'

Intrigued by Edison's development of the light bulb, the British parliament established a committee to look at its potential in 1878. The committee concluded that the light bulb was 'good enough for our transatlantic cousins ... but unworthy of the attention of practical or scientific men'.

'That rainbow song is no good. Take it out.'

MGM INTERNAL MEMO AFTER THE INITIAL SCREENING
OF *THE WIZARD OF OZ*

On 3 October 1995 media outlets across the world were vying to be the first to announce the result of the infamous O. J. Simpson trial. All of them announced the surprise 'Not guilty' verdict except the Time Warner Pathfinder website, which splashed 'Guilty!' across its home page.

'I tell you, Wellington is a bad general. The English are bad soldiers; we will settle the matter by lunchtime.'

NAPOLEON ON THE EVE OF HIS DEFEAT AT THE
BATTLE OF WATERLOO

'You will be home before the leaves have fallen from the trees.'

KAISER WILHELM II IN AUGUST 1914 TO HIS TROOPS AT THE
START OF WORLD WAR I, WHICH WENT ON FOR FOUR YEARS

FAIL

'No matter what happens, the US Navy is not going to be caught napping.'

FRANK KNOX, US SECRETARY OF THE NAVY, 4 DECEMBER 1941,
JUST THREE DAYS BEFORE THE JAPANESE LAUNCHED THEIR
DEVASTATING SURPRISE ATTACK ON PEARL HARBOR

'Don't worry about it. It's nothing.'

US NAVY LIEUTENANT KERMIT TYLER ON 7 DECEMBER 1941, AFTER
BEING TOLD THAT RADAR WAS SHOWING A HUGE FORMATION OF
PLANES HEADING FOR HAWAII. IT WAS, OF COURSE, THE FIRST
WAVE OF JAPANESE PLANES ABOUT TO ATTACK PEARL HARBOR

In 1886 a gold prospector named Sors Hariezon sold a claim he had made on a farm in Witwatersrand in the Transvaal. He was glad to take £10 for it and moved on. For the next 90 years, gold mines on or near his claim produced over a million kilos of gold a year – over 70 per cent of the Western world's gold supply.

FAIL

Dr Stuart M. Berger was a renowned author and dietician who promoted the fact that his weight-loss programmes would result in living longer. He died in February 1994 aged 40, weighing 26 stone.

When Alexander Graham Bell invented the telephone in 1876, he took it to Western Union, who then ran all the telegraph lines in America. They wrote back saying, 'After careful consideration of your invention, which is a very interesting novelty, we have come to the conclusion that it has no commercial potential.' Bell's patent for the telephone went on to become the most valuable patent in history.

FAIL

THEY CALLED IT WRONG

'You ain't going nowhere.
You ought to go back to driving a truck!'

JIM DENNY, MANAGER OF THE GRAND OLE OPRY,
TO A STRUGGLING MUSICIAN WHO'D JUST PERFORMED AT
HIS VENUE IN 1954. THE SINGER WAS ELVIS PRESLEY

'Who the hell wants to hear actors talk?'

HARRY WARNER, WARNER BROS, 1926

FAIL

'The band's OK, but if I were you, I'd get rid of the
singer with the tyre-tread lips.'

BBC RADIO PRODUCER, REJECTING THE ROLLING STONES
AT A 1963 AUDITION

189

'I cannot imagine any condition which would cause a ship to flounder. Modern shipbuilding has gone beyond that.'

CAPTAIN EDWARD J. SMITH, COMMANDER OF THE *TITANIC*

FAIL

'Shows no promise.'

MUNICH TECHNICAL INSTITUTE REJECTING A YOUNG STUDENT CALLED ALBERT EINSTEIN IN 1898

'Nuclear plants, like colour TV sets, give off minute amounts of radiation.'

COLUMN BY *NEWSWEEK* JOURNALIST GEORGE WILL. THE NEXT DAY THE THREE MILE ISLAND NUCLEAR FACILITY IN PENNSYLVANIA BROKE DOWN, NEARLY CAUSING A NUCLEAR DISASTER

FAIL

'The Internet will collapse within a year.'

BOB METCALF, FOUNDER OF 3COM, DECEMBER 1995

Darryl F. Zanuck, founder of 20th Century Film, later to become 20th Century Fox, didn't enjoy a good record for recognizing star quality. Actors he rejected in his career included Cary Grant, Fred Astaire, Errol Flynn and Clark Gable, of whom he said, 'His ears are too big. He looks like an ape.'

FAIL

Intel co-founder and chairman Gordon Moore was presented with the idea of a personal computer in the early 1970s and had just four words to say about it: 'What's it good for?'

'Forget *Gone with the Wind*, Lou. No Civil War picture ever made a nickel.'

PRODUCER IRVING THALBERG IN 1936 TO LOUIS B. MAYER

[FAIL]

'Sean Connery can't play the sophisticated James Bond. He looks like a bricklayer.'

PRODUCERS OF THE FIRST JAMES BOND MOVIE, *DR NO* (THEY WANTED JAMES MASON OR CARY GRANT TO STAR IN THE MOVIE)

When Christopher Columbus first proposed to search for a shorter route to the Indies, a report was commissioned by the court of King Ferdinand V and Queen Isabella of Spain. It concluded, 'So many centuries after creation it is unlikely that anyone could find hitherto unknown lands of any value.'

[FAIL]

'We don't need you. You haven't gone through college yet.'

HEWLETT PACKARD EXECUTIVE REJECTING STEVE JOBS AND STEVE WOZNIAK AND THEIR NEW APPLE PERSONAL COMPUTER. THE REST, AS THEY SAY, IS HISTORY

In 1995 opera singer Luciano Pavarotti described his marriage to his wife, Adua, as 'incredibly monogamous'. Less than six months later he admitted having an affair with a 26-year-old assistant.

FAIL

In 1995 actress Pamela Anderson said that her marriage to rock star Tommy Lee was the 'best thing I've ever done in my whole life'. A year later she filed for divorce. Someone else who didn't quite get it right was Britt Ekland, who confidently announced in 1976 that husband Rod Stewart 'will stay with me forever'. They divorced the following year.

'Atomic energy might be as good as our present-day explosives, but it is unlikely to produce anything very much more dangerous.'

WINSTON CHURCHILL, 1939

FAIL

'The cinema is little more than a fad. It's canned drama. What audiences really want to see is flesh and blood on the stage.'

CHARLIE CHAPLIN, 1916

'For the majority of people, the use of tobacco has a beneficial effect.'

IAN MACDONALD, LOS ANGELES SURGEON, QUOTED IN *NEWSWEEK*, 1963

'I have no enemies. Why should I fear?'

US PRESIDENT WILLIAM MCKINLEY, AUGUST 1901, A FEW DAYS
BEFORE HIS ASSASSINATION

'You can't say the people of Dallas haven't given
you a nice welcome.'

MRS JOHN CONNALLY, WIFE OF THE GOVERNOR OF TEXAS TO
JOHN F. KENNEDY JUST PRIOR TO HIS ASSASSINATION

[FAIL]

'Sensible and responsible women do not want to vote.'

FORMER PRESIDENT GROVER CLEVELAND, 1900

'An island of stability.'

PRESIDENT JIMMY CARTER IN 1979 DESCRIBING
THE SHAH OF IRAN. HE WAS DEPOSED A FEW MONTHS
LATER AND FLED THE COUNTRY

[FAIL]

Writing and rejection go hand-in-hand, as these *Epic Fail* decisions show...

J. K. Rowling
Harry Potter and the Philosopher's Stone was rejected by a raft of publishers. It was eventually taken up by Bloomsbury, a small London publisher, after its CEO was persuaded to publish it by his insistent eight-year-old daughter.

George Orwell
One publisher rejected *Animal Farm* on the basis that 'it is impossible to sell animal stories in the USA.'

John le Carré
His first novel, *The Spy Who Came in from the Cold*, was rejected by one editor, who passed it to a colleague with the message, 'You're welcome to le Carré. He hasn't got any future.'

Anne Frank
Fifteen publishers turned down *The Diary of Anne Frank*. One publisher claimed it was hardly worth reading, stating than Anne didn't 'have a special perception or feeling which would lift the book above "curiosity value"'.

Joseph Heller
One publisher who turned down *Catch-22* wrote: 'I haven't the foggiest idea about what the man is trying to say.'

Stephen King
His first novel, *Carrie*, was rejected 30 times with one of the publishers commenting, 'We are not interested in science fiction which deals with negative utopias. They do not sell.'

William Golding
Lord of the Flies was rejected by 20 publishers. One described this future classic as 'an absurd and uninteresting fantasy, which was rubbish and dull.'

Rudyard Kipling
An editor who rejected one of his short stories did so with the note, 'I'm sorry, Mr Kipling, but you just don't know how to use the English language.'

Frank Herbert

His epic novel *Dune* was rejected 23 times before being published and being widely acclaimed as one of the most loved and innovative science fiction novels of all time.

Jack Kerouac

A rejection for *On the Road* commented, 'His frenetic and scrambled prose perfectly express the feverish travels of the Beat Generation, but is that enough? I don't think so.'

Kenneth Grahame

Wind in the Willows was rejected on the grounds that it was 'an irresponsible holiday story'.

D. H. Lawrence

After reading *Lady Chatterley's Lover*, one publisher gave the author this sage piece of advice: 'For your own sake do not publish this book.'

F. Scott Fitzgerald

One editor told him, 'You'd have a decent book if you'd get rid of that Gatsby character.'

FAIL

THE FUTURE'S BRIGHT...
BUT THE PREDICTIONS
WEREN'T

> *'If at first you don't succeed, find out if the loser gets anything.'*
>
> BILL LYON

The examples in this chapter prove you should never make predictions, especially about the future...

'Everything that can be invented, has been invented.'

CHARLES DUELL, COMMISSIONER OF THE US PATENT OFFICE, 1899

'Heavier-than-air flying machines are impossible.'

LORD KELVIN, PRESIDENT OF THE ROYAL SOCIETY, IN 1895

'I think there is a world market for maybe five computers.'

THOMAS WATSON, IBM CHAIRMAN, 1943

'Television won't last because people will soon get tired of staring at a plywood box every night.'

DARYL ZANUCK, MOVIE PRODUCER AT 20TH CENTURY FOX, 1946

FAIL

'Airplanes are interesting toys but of no military value.'

MARÉCHAL FERDINAND FOCH, WAR STRATEGIST, IN 1911

'Computers in the future may weigh no more than 1.5 tons.'

ARTICLE IN POPULAR MECHANICS MAGAZINE, 1949

FAIL

'There is no reason anyone would want a computer in their home.'

KEN OLSEN, CEO OF DIGITAL EQUIPMENT CORPORATION, 1977

On 17 October 1929, Irving Fisher, Yale University professor of economics, stated that 'stocks have reached what looks like a permanently high plateau'. The Wall Street Crash followed one week later.

The year before, Thomas Watson, the founder of IBM, confidently stated: 'We may look with confidence to the progress of business in 1929.'

FAIL

'Human beings in the future will become one-toed. The small toes are being used less and less as time goes on, while the great toe is developing in an astonishing manner.'

RICHARD LUCAS, ROYAL COLLEGE OF SURGEONS, 1911

'Television won't last. It's a flash in the pan.'

MARY SOMMERVILLE, RADIO BROADCASTER, 1948

[FAIL]

'Nuclear-powered vacuum cleaners will probably
be a reality in ten years.'

ALEX LEWYT, PRESIDENT OF LEWYT CORP, MANUFACTURERS
OF VACUUM CLEANERS, IN 1955

'Brain-work will cause her to become bald, while increasing
masculinity and contempt for beauty will induce the growth
of hair on her face. In the future, therefore, women will be
bald and wear long moustaches and patriarchal beards.'

PROFESSOR HANS FRIEDENTHAL OF BERLIN UNIVERSITY
ON THE EVOLUTION OF WOMEN AFTER HIGHER EDUCATION AND
VOTING RIGHTS, 1914

[FAIL]

'When the housewife of 2000 cleans house she simply turns
the hose on everything. Why not? Furniture, rugs, draperies,
unscratchable floors are all made of synthetic fabric or
waterproof plastic. After the water has run down a drain in
the middle of the floor (later concealed by a rug of synthetic
fibre), she turns on a blast of hot air and dries everything.'

POPULAR MECHANICS, 1950

'There will be no C, Q or X in our everyday alphabet.
They will be abandoned because unnecessary.'

JOHN WATKINS JR WRITING IN THE LADIES' HOME JOURNAL, 1900

FAIL

'Inventions reached their limit long ago and I see no hope
for future development.'

JULIUS FRONTINUS, FIRST CENTURY AD

'Rail travel at high speeds is not possible because
passengers, unable to breathe, would die of asphyxia.'

DIONYSIUS LARDNER, C.1835, IRISH ASTRONOMER
AND PHILOSOPHER

FAIL

'I must confess that my imagination refuses to see
any sort of submarine doing anything but suffocating
its crew and floundering at sea.'

VISIONARY SCIENCE FICTION WRITER H. G. WELLS, 1901

'The popular mind often pictures gigantic flying machines
speeding across the Atlantic, carrying innumerable
passengers. Such ideas must be wholly visionary. Even if
such a machine could get across with one or two
passengers, it would be prohibitive to any but the capitalist
who could own his own yacht.'

WILLIAM PICKERING, HARVARD ASTRONOMER, 1913

'No flying machine will ever fly from New York to Paris.'

ORVILLE WRIGHT, 1908

'Automobiles will start to decline almost as soon as the last shot is fired in the Second World War. Instead of a car in every garage, there will be a helicopter.'

AVIATION PUBLICIST HARRY BRUNO, 1943

FAIL

The grandly named Richard van der Riet Woolley was Astronomer Royal and space advisor to the British Government, so you'd think he'd have a little bit more foresight when he announced in 1956 that 'space travel is utter bilge'.

A year later Russia launched its successful Sputnik satellite.

A Short History of the Future was written by John Langdon-Davies in 1936, and contained these predictions:

- There will be no war in Western Europe in the next five years.

- Crime will be considered a disease after 1985 and will cease to exist by 1990.

- Democracy will be dead by 1950.

The Amazing Criswell was a syndicated American television psychic from the 1950s and 1960s with a difference: he was renowned for his wildly inaccurate predictions. Born Jeron Criswell King, he was a flamboyant character who claimed to sleep in a coffin, appeared in a sequinned tuxedo and spoke in a loud, booming voice. Criswell's predictions included:

- An outbreak of cannibalism across Pittsburgh in 1980.

- London being wiped out by a meteor strike in October 1988.

- Every woman in a 'major American city' losing her hair.

- America being engulfed by a mysterious aphrodisiac cloud resulting in its borders being closed to prevent people getting in and taking advantage of the nation's uncontrollable sexual urges.

- A nudism movement spreading across the country from Rhode Island that would 'make the hippie movement look normal'.

- Geological changes that would turn Manhattan into the Venice of the eastern seaboard.

- The end of the world on 18 August 1999 – a day where every point on earth would be covered by a black rainbow that will suck the oxygen from the air.

Criswell was good friends with actress Mae West and became her personal psychic. He predicted that she would become President of the United States, at which point she, Criswell and George Liberace, the brother of pianist and showman Liberace, would take a rocket to the moon.

TECHNOLOGY GONE WRONG

'We have forty million reasons for failure, but not a single excuse.'

RUDYARD KIPLING

When it comes to technology, it's almost a rule of law that if it can go wrong, it will. Try and make something idiot-proof and someone will just make a better idiot...

[FAIL]

It's all in the detail – which is something those behind NASA's Mariner 1 space probe should have borne in mind. A minus sign omitted from its flight programme meant that instead of a 100-day trip to Venus, it plunged into the Atlantic Ocean just four minutes after take-off in July 1962.

Similarly, in 1999 a stupid error in the software code of the Mars Polar Lander made it think it had landed when in fact it was actually 130 feet above the planet's surface. The $110 million (£68.6 million) spacecraft shut down its engines early and crashed into Mars.

In October 1994 the Intel Corporation was informed there was a fault in its latest Pentium P5 chip and its executives admitted they had been aware of this since May that year. The story appeared in the press in November, with Intel claiming the problem would only affect one in every nine billion calculations. In reality the problem occurred a lot more frequently – as often as every 24 days, according to IBM – and Intel customers halted shipments of computers installed with these chips. In December Intel finally succumbed to public outcry and bad publicity and offered to replace all the faulty chips – at a reported cost of $475 million (£296.5 million).

In 1987 Motorola engineers came up with a solution to the poor and patchy mobile phone service that existed in the US. The idea involved putting 66 new satellites into earth orbit providing a 24-hour wireless phone service all over the world. The project was called Iridium; Motorola invested $2.5 billion (£1.6 billion) into it and encouraged other investors to add an additional $2.5 billion. When the service went live in 1999 it promised subscribers the ability to talk 'with anyone, anytime, virtually anywhere in the world'.

The downside of Motorola's new service was that the phones cost $3,000 (£1,900), were as bulky as 'brick' mobile phones from 15 years earlier – and could not work indoors. The company had predicted 1.6 million subscribers by 2000; its peak figure was 55,000. A year after the launch the whole project went bankrupt.

Necdet Bakimci, a Syrian lorry driver, set out from Antakya in Turkey in 2008 to deliver his car transporter loaded with luxury vehicles to Coral Road, Gibraltar. Relying on his satnav he in fact ended up 1,600 miles adrift at Gibraltar Point Nature Reserve near Skegness.

Not as extreme but equally alarming was the case of the two Swedish holidaymakers who wanted to reach the picturesque Italian island of Capri but instead typed 'Carpi' in their satnav. They ended up in an industrial town nearly 400 miles away. A Carpi local government spokesman commented, 'It's hard to understand how they managed it. I mean, Capri is an island.'

OneNewsNow.com, the website from the fundamentalist Christian American Family Association, operates an automatic filter to change words that 'do not suit' its ideological line. However, this attracted ridicule once it started carrying news about the American sprinter Tyson Gay. In a report on his 2008 Beijing Olympics qualifying trials the site's filter automatically changed his surname to Homosexual.

The website's report included the text: 'Tyson Homosexual was a blur in blue, sprinting 100 meters faster than anyone ever has', and '"It means a lot to me," the 25-year-old Homosexual said. "I'm glad my body could do it, because now I know I have it in me."'

These reports took first place in a 2009 award for Best American Censorship Blunder.

[FAIL]

It was difficult for scientists working at the SETI Institute (The Search for Extra Terrestrial Intelligence) to contain their excitement when the Parkes Observatory in Australia began picking up what seemed like an intelligent signal from space. The signal was loud and clear and happened at 7 pm every day.

In January 1996, after comprehensive investigations, SETI's Dr Peter Backus announced the results to an expectant audience of the American Astronomical Society in Texas. To their dismay, however, he apologetically explained that the signal was in fact emanating from a microwave oven in the observatory's kitchen. He sheepishly told them, 'We thought it was odd that this only happened at mealtimes.' (There is now a note on the microwave asking technicians not to use it when SETI is active.)

A passenger caused chaos on a packed Tokyo commuter train when his rubber underpants suddenly inflated to 30 times their original size. The underpants were his own invention, designed to protect the wearer from drowning in the event of a tidal wave reaching the Japanese mainland, but a technical fault caused their premature inflation. His fellow commuters were only saved from being crushed in the crowded carriage by a quick-thinking passenger, who burst them with a sharp pencil.

Austrian Franz Reichelt was known as the Flying Tailor – an inaccurate nickname as he plunged rather than flew from the Eiffel Tower to his death when demonstrating his 'parachute suit' in 1912. Reichelt was obsessed with developing a suit for aviators that would transform into a parachute if they ever needed to jump from their aircraft. Getting permission from the Parisian police, he climbed the Eiffel Tower wearing one of the suits and leaped from the first stage. The parachute coat failed to work and, captured on film, he crashed into the icy ground at the foot of the tower, suffering a gruesome and instant death.

FAIL

When NASA launched the $1.6 billion (£1 billion) Hubble telescope into space in April 1990, it discovered that the main mirror had been ground to the wrong shape, making images blurred. To save money NASA had decided not to run diagnostic tests on the telescope before its launch. If it had, then the lens could have been corrected on earth at a cost of $2 million (£1.25 million). Instead, a special space shuttle mission was launched in 1993 to fit the telescope with a corrective lens – at a cost of $86 million (£53.7 million).

When it was introduced in Hong Kong, a mechanical arm-wrestling machine managed to break the arms of five men in a two-week period. Although the arcade game, Arm Champs II, did warn players that they took part at their own risk, the signs were in English and most of those playing were young Chinese.

FAIL

Customers couldn't believe their eyes when they went into their Pak 'n' Save supermarket in Hamilton, New Zealand, in April 2011 only to find it completely empty of security guards, sales assistants and cashiers. While a few citizens paid for their groceries using the self-checkouts, most took advantage of the situation and left without paying. It turned out the supermarket shouldn't have been open at all. It was Good Friday and a security system computer glitch was blamed for the doors opening and the lights coming on for more than eight hours from 1 am. According to the *Waikato Times*, the free-for-all ended when someone rang police saying people were leaving the shop with 'truckloads of groceries'.

Embarrassed supermarket owner Glenn Miller said he did not know how much stock was taken but he was delighted that 12 honest people had used the self-service tills to pay for items.

During the 1960s Space Race it's reported that NASA spent in the region of $1.5 million (£.94 million) developing a ballpoint pen that would write in a vacuum, in zero gravity and in extremes of hot and cold. The Russians were faced with the same dilemma. They used pencils.

William Bullock was the American inventor of the rotary printing press, a revolutionary design that allowed large rolls of paper to be fed through the rollers instead of laboriously hand-feeding separate sheets. One day in April 1867, Bullock kicked one of his machines in frustration and his foot became caught in the machinery and severely mangled. A few days later the wound developed gangrene and he died during an operation to amputate his leg.

BEWARE THE WARNING!

> *'Success is the one unpardonable sin against one's fellows.'*
>
> AMBROSE BIERCE

Warning: *If you have to rely on the advice given on the following products' labels or packaging, then you're an idiot.*

'Not to be used for anything else.'

JAPANESE FOOD PROCESSOR

'Do not iron clothes on body.'

ROWENTA IRON

'Do not use to pick up anything that is burning.'

UNKNOWN BRAND VACUUM CLEANER

'Warning: May cause drowsiness.'

NYTOL SLEEP AID

FAIL

'Wearing of this garment does not enable you to fly.'

CHILD-SIZED SUPERMAN COSTUME

☹

'Instructions: Open packet. Eat nuts.'

AMERICAN AIRLINES PEANUTS

FAIL

'Product will be hot after heating.'

MARKS & SPENCER'S BREAD PUDDING

☹

'Do not turn upside down.'
[Printed on the bottom of the packet.]

TESCO'S TIRAMISU DESSERT

FAIL

'Warning. This product contains nuts.'

SAINSBURY'S PEANUTS

☹

'For best results, remove cap.'

NABISCO EASY CHEESE

'Do not eat packet.'

HORMEL PEPPERONI

[FAIL]

'Do not take if allergic to aspirin.'

BAYER ASPIRIN

'Ingredient: Sugar.'

DOMINO PURE CANE GRANULATED SUGAR

[FAIL]

'Do not take if allergic to Zantac.'

ZANTAC 75

'Note: Game pieces do not actually talk.'

'GUESS WHO?' GAME

☹

'Warning: Contents may be hot.'

MCDONALD'S COFFEE

FAIL

'This ice may be cold.'

SLUSH PUPPY CUP

☹

'Warning: Remove label before placing in microwave.'

MOËT WHITE STAR CHAMPAGNE

FAIL

'Caution: Do not use near power lines.'

UNKNOWN BRAND TOILET PLUNGER

☹

'Do not attempt to stop chain with hands.'

JONSERED'S CHAINSAW

FAIL

'All divers must land in water!'

SIGN ON DIVING BOARD

'Warning: For indoor or outdoor use only.'

UNKNOWN CHRISTMAS LIGHTS

'Warning: Do not attempt to swallow.'

UNKNOWN MATTRESS

'Safe to use around pets.'

ARM & HAMMER SCOOPABLE CAT LITTER

'This product is not defined as flammable by the Consumer Products Safety Commission Regulations. However, this product can be ignited under certain circumstances.'

ENDUST DUSTER

'Do not drive a car or run machinery.'

BOOT'S CHILDREN'S COUGH MEDICINE

THE WORST OF
THE WORST

> *'If all else fails, immortality can always be assured by spectacular error.'*
>
> JOHN KENNETH GALBRAITH

Just because a failure can't be categorized doesn't make it any less ironic, humorous or humiliating...

> FAIL

During the 1979 UK docks strike, pickets arrived very early one morning to set up their demonstration outside the large iron gates of Immingham Dock near Grimsby. It was only when it became light that they discovered they were actually picketing the town cemetery.

☹

On 22 April 1990 an estimated 750,000 people gathered in New York's Central Park to celebrate Earth Day and raise awareness of the environmental, issues affecting the planet. They left behind 154 tons of litter.

> FAIL

A 'Geographical Agent and Broker Listing' in *Business Insurance Magazine* got its countries a bit mixed up. According to the feature, Aberdeen was in Saudi Arabia, Antwerp was in Barbados, Belfast was in Nigeria, Helsinki was in Fiji, Moscow was in Qatar and Cardiff was in Vietnam.

FAIL

Gabrielle Schmitt decided that her psychology degree project would be to investigate the effect of nagging. For a test subject she rented a room in her apartment to carpenter Andi Weber and proceeded to nag him day and night about anything she could think of, just to monitor his reaction. After weeks of nagging he snapped, battering Gabrielle's head with an axe.

Andi was given a lenient four-year prison sentence due to the fact that he was provoked.

In 1991 the book *Looking Forward* by President George H. W. Bush earned $2,718 (£1,700) in royalties. A book 'written' by the family dog, *Millie's Book*, ghost-written by First Lady Barbara Bush, earned $889,176 (£555,270).

FAIL

Expectations were high when it was announced that in October 1992 wilderness expert Alistair Emms was going to talk to 260 pupils at the clifftop Allhallows School, near Seaton, south Devon, about how to survive in the wild.

Mr Emms arrived early and decided to go for a walk. However, when he failed to return after an hour staff became concerned and called the emergency services. The coastguard was alerted, but after they failed to locate any sign of him police and two auxiliary coastguard units were called in. Soon the search involved 40 local people, five police officers, a tracker dog and two helicopters.

After five hours Mr Emms was located, stranded on a cliff edge. A police spokesman said: 'He just wanted to stay there and come down when he was ready. Eventually he was talked into getting winched into the helicopter.'

The lecture was never delivered and the school decided not to invite him back.

In May 2001 a case involving two staff injured while they were stuck between floors in a hospital elevator was scheduled to be held at the Westchester County Courthouse in White Plains, New York. Unfortunately, the jury on their way to hear the case got stuck in the courthouse lift themselves. The defense attorney argued that this unexpected event might prejudice the jury. The judge agreed and declared a mistrial – and a new jury was selected.

[FAIL]

Criminal Mike Stacey was on the run after failing to pay a US court the equivalent of £10,000 in fines for selling counterfeit T-shirts. Rather than lie low he decided to enter the US version of *Who Wants to Be a Millionaire?* He was spotted by a local policeman and arrested as soon as he left the studio. To add insult to injury he failed to win any money.

In a similar story, Brazilian Vincente Brito de Queiroz appeared in person on TV to collect his $5 million (£3.12 million) lottery winnings from the state lottery – and was immediately identified by police as an escaped fugitive wanted for questioning in connection with the death of his wife.

In 1974, Basil Brown, a 48-year-old health-food advocate from Croydon, drank himself to death with carrot juice. Over a period of ten days it's estimated he drank 10 gallons of carrot juice that gave him 10,000 times the recommended amount of vitamin A. He died from irreversible liver damage.

☹

Bosses at the Volvo GM Heavy Truck Corporation in Dublin, Virginia, came up with an ingenious way to shame late workers into turning up on time. They assigned an employee to dress up as a giant rooster and when someone clocked in late for their shift, he would sneak up behind them and yell, 'Cock-a-doodle-do!'

Marshall Lineberry didn't appreciate this reaction when he arrived late for his shift so he grabbed the rooster and started to choke it before being pulled away by colleagues. Volvo GM suspended him but he was reinstated after a court found that the rooster's act amounted to provocation.

FAIL

Mr Bob Sower, an entomologist from Oregon, was involved in an extensive study to develop an artificial sex attractant for Tussock moths to assist in their breeding. After a long day in the lab he went straight to a night baseball game without going home first for his customary shower. As the match went on Mr Sower found himself the centre of attention for what seemed like all the Tussock moths in Oregon and had to be eventually rescued by other spectators.

One of his rescuers commented that with the thousands of moths covering Mr Sower, he looked like a puffball. 'When we managed to get through to him his suit was quite eaten away and half his hair was gone.'

Pride of place in County Durham local history museum was a pristine Roman coin. It had been on display for some time until 1971 when an observant primary school pupil, Fiona Gordon, who was just nine years old, recognized it as being a plastic token from a soft drinks company. The museum had interpreted the distinctive 'R' on the coin as meaning 'Rome' when in fact it stood for the famous producer of lemon barley water, Robinsons.

Actor Tony Randall, spokesman for National Sleep Disorder Month, failed to turn up on the TV show *Wake Up America*. He overslept.

The unfortunately named Grant Shittit of Timaru, New Zealand, staggered home after a heavy night and, overcome by fatigue, decided to lie down in a soft bed of cool moss. On waking the next morning he discovered that the moss had actually been wet cement that had set during the night, trapping him. Only able to move his head, he lay there for 72 hours until he was spotted by a passing motorist, and eventually freed by firemen. A now-sober Shittit commented, 'It was particularly uncomfortable because I'd been sick on myself in the night.'

FAIL

Japanese petty crook Wang Woo threw himself off the top of his ten-storey Tokyo apartment building in the mistaken belief that his son's *Postman Pat* video contained subliminal threats from the Yakuza, the Japanese mafia. Postman Pat only has three fingers, a feature shared by ruthless Yakuza members who amputate a finger to prove their loyalty to the organization. According to his wife, 36-year-old Mr Woo turned white as soon as she saw his son's video, screaming, 'The bastards have found me at last!' and every time Pat waved at the camera, 'He squealed like a piglet.' Scared out of his wits, Woo then threw himself out of his apartment window.

Adam Zebrak was looking to buy an antique cigarette lighter at a sensible price at an auction in Sussex when a wasp flew into his shirt just as the bidding began. The auctioneer took his wild, flailing arm movements as an indication of his bids, and the price was pushed higher and higher. It reached £500 when the rival bidder dropped out and Zebrak was forced to buy the lighter at this massively inflated sum.

Organizers of the 1985 annual conference of the Association of British Travel Agents (ABTA) wanted to make a good impression on all its delegates, reinforcing the view that British travel agents were among the best in the world when it came to organizing holidays and itineraries.

The event in Sorrento, Italy, failed to get off to a good start when fog at Gatwick delayed flights, ensuring that most people arrived a day late. Food poisoning was rife and a leading delegate was bitten by a snake. Those looking forward to the conference golf tournament were severely disappointed, as organizers had failed to realize there was no golf course in Sorrento. The climax was an address by the Italian Minister of Development in the forum at Pompeii, which was to include 3,500 roses being dropped by a plane over the delegates. No one could hear the closing speech due to the aircraft noise – it had to make five passes to get into the right position to drop the roses – and even then it missed the forum completely.

Labour MP Rhodri Morgan was appearing on BBC Radio Wales in 1993 to extol the virtues of the country's electricity supply and its impressive record for continuity of supply, unlike many other countries where blackouts were commonplace. He was cut off in mid-flow when a power cut temporarily took the station off the air.

ACKNOWLEDGEMENTS

The author would like to thank the following people for either their guidance, helpful suggestions or for just keeping out of my damn way while I was writing this bloody book:

Hannah Knowles, Darin Jewel, Barney Leigh, Debbie Leigh, Polly Leigh, Kate Moore & Maxwell Woofington III

BIBLIOGRAPHY

Wrong! by Jane O'Boyle (Plume)

On Second Thoughts by Gary Belsky (Michael O'Mara)

I Wish I Hadn't Said That Edited by Christopher Cerf and Victor Navasky (Harper Collins)

They Got It Wrong! The Guinness Book of Regrettable Quotations Compiled by David Milsted (Guinness Publishing)

Dumb, Dumber, Dumbest by John J. Kohut & Roland Sweet (Plume)

They Didn't Really Mean It by Russell Ash & Bernard Higton (Corgi)

World Famous Mistakes by Esme Hawes & Jesse Flowerfoot (Magpie Books)

The Stupidest Things Ever Said Book of All-Time Stupidest Top Ten Lists by Kathryn & Ross Petras (Workman Publishing)

Enormous Books by Stewart Ferris (Summersdale)

Celebrities Behaving Badly by Carol McGiffin & Mark Leigh (Summersdale)

The Ultimate Book of Heroic Failures by Stephen Pile (Faber & Faber)

The Lexicon of Stupidity by Ross & Kathryn Petras (Workman Publishing)

Knuckleheads in the News by John Machay (Ballantine Books)

Tarrant on Millionaires by Chris Tarrant (Harper Collins)

True Animal Tales by Rolf Harris (Century)

Beasty Behaviour by Rolf Harris (Century)

Complete and Utter Failure by Neil Steinberg (Pavilion Books)

Stupid Things Men Do by Andrew John (Michael o'Mara)

The World's Worst by Mark Frauenfelder (Chronicle Books)

The Fortean Times Book of Life's Losers compiled by Ian Simmons (John Brown Publishing)

Dear Valued Customer, You Are A Loser by Rick Broadhead (Andrews McMeel Publishing)

The Darwin Awards by Wendy Northcutt (Orion)

Great British Losers by Gordon Kerr (Old Street Publishing)

George W. Bushisms edited by Jacob Weisberg (Fireside)

The Bumper Book of Erotic Failures by Dr Peter Kinnell (Warner Books)

Great Commercial Disasters by Stephen Winkworth (Macmillan)

The World's Stupidest Deaths by Andrew John & Stephen Blake (Michael O'Mara)

The Fortean Times Book of Inept Crime compiled by Steve Moore (John Brown Publishing)

Death by Spaghetti edited by Paul Sussman (Fourth Estate)

The Best Book of Bizarre But True Stories Ever by Mike Flynn (Carlton Books)

1001 Ridiculous Sexual Misadventures by Gina McKinnon (Prion)

Would You Believe It? by Philip Mason (Futura)